Strategies
for Training
Housing Managers

Sue Farrant
Karen Mullan
Euan Ramsay

Chartered Institute of Housing

The Chartered Institute of Housing

The Chartered Institute of Housing is the professional organisation for all people who work in housing. Its purpose is to take a strategic and leading role in encouraging and promoting the provision of good quality affordable housing for all. The Institute has more than 11,000 members working in local authorities, housing associations, the private sector and educational institutions.

Chartered Institute of Housing
Octavia House
Westwood Way
Coventry CV4 8JP
Telephone: 0203 694433

Strategies for Training Housing Managers

Authors: Sue Farrant, Karen Mullan and Euan Ramsay

© Chartered Institute of Housing 1994

Published by the Chartered Institute of Housing

ISBN 0 901607 75 4

Graphic design by Henry's House Design Co–operative Ltd.
Printed by Warwick Printing Co. Ltd.

Contents

Good practice examples

About the authors

Sue Farrant and Karen Mullan were senior consultants with Aldbourne Associates when this work was commissioned. They have since established The FM Partnership in order to specialise in the writing, editing and production of manuals, handbooks and other informative material. Sue is the principal author of *Managing Neighbour Complaints in Social Housing: A Handbook for Practitioners* (Aldbourne Associates, 1993).

Euan Ramsay, a senior consultant with Aldbourne Associates, has worked in social housing for more than twenty years. He is the principal author of *Education and Training for Housing Management*, DOE, 1994.

Aldbourne Associates is a management consultancy specialising in social housing. The practice carries out research and consultancy for government, local authority, housing association and voluntary sector organisations and currently has a client base of over seventy organisations.

Acknowledgements

Many people and organisations have generously given time, advice and material to the authors as this book has been prepared and we are very grateful to them all. Our particular thanks go to:

Cathy Mullan, Western Health and Social Services Board, Northern Ireland

Kate Hargreaves, HERA

Suzie Scott, University of Glasgow

John Swanton, Waverley Borough Council

The Local Government Management Board

The housing organisations which contributed examples of good practice. They are listed by name in Appendix 1.

Glossary

Defining Terms

Training, like any other field of activity, has its own jargon which is often difficult for the non–specialist to get to grips with. To make matters worse, technical words are often used with slightly different meanings by different people! So that users of this publication can start from a common point, there follows a list of the main terms used with a brief definition of what we intend them to mean.

Education
Study over varying periods, most commonly at educational colleges and institutions, with a housing qualification as the ultimate goal.

Effectiveness
Having the desired result. Measures of effectiveness must be determined before training is undertaken. Both individual and organisation will have views on what the desired result of any given training activity is to be and these views might not overlap entirely.

Efficiency
The ratio of useful outcomes to the total resources put in. An efficient training programme is one where maximum return is gained from the investment of a given level of resources. Resources are not, of course, simply monetary; time is a resource which is usually in short supply. Neither are outcomes necessarily tangible. A course intended to teach rent accounting might also have an unplanned, but valuable, team building effect.

Evaluation
Assessment or appraisal of the total costs and benefits (financial, managerial and social) of a piece of training or training programme. The evaluation of process and output should follow any training activity and requires careful preparation and follow up.

Housing management
In this book the term housing management refers exclusively to the management and servicing of homes owned by social housing organisations. The central tasks covered by this definition are lettings, rents, property and estate management, maintenance and repairs, dealing with tenants and tenancies, research and development and administration.

Knowledge
Defined as the possession of information about a topic. Knowledge can be entirely theoretical.

Skill
The ability to perform a particular task. A skill is the practical application of a particular, and sometimes very limited, aspect of knowledge.

Social Housing Organisations
Housing associations, local authorities, and other public bodies which own housing stock, as well as organisations which manage stock owned by HAs, LAs or other public bodies.

Training
Planned activities which are intended to teach skills, knowledge or attitudes which are of direct application to the work environment. Training may be delivered in many ways, ranging from formal courses to 'learning by doing'.

Training Plan
A document which sets out the organisation's goals and detailed strategy for training its personnel over a defined period of time. Individuals within the organisation might also have individual training plans which map out their career development.

Training Policy
A statement of intent about how the housing department or housing association intends to manage training. The organisation's training policies will largely determine the content of the training plan.

Validation
Checking that a training programme or training event has met its declared objectives. This would normally be part of the evaluation process.

Chapter 1
Introduction

1.1   Why manage training?

This is a period of rapid change for the social housing sector. Not only is the legislative and policy framework changing, but so too are the expectations of customers. Local authorities, the major managers and providers of social rented housing for the last fifty or more years, are now becoming strategic planning and enabling organisations. Their housing management functions will be opened up to compulsory competitive tendering (CCT) and a number of authorities have explored, or are exploring, various options, including the transfer of stock to housing associations. Housing associations themselves are being promoted as the developers and managers of social rented housing for all sectors of the community.

At the same time, the practices and procedures of housing management are undergoing change, with greater involvement by customers in the services provided, an increasing emphasis on value for money in the resources committed to housing and changes in the structures and operating methods of housing organisations.

It seems that nothing can be taken for granted any more! As the goal posts move, the successful teams will be the ones whose players are able to adapt rapidly to changing circumstances whilst working efficiently and effectively as one body. This applies to the profession as a whole, as much as to individual housing organisations, making it essential to review continuously both the professional education of housing managers and the training provided by social housing organisations to their staff at all levels.

This handbook was commissioned by the Chartered Institute of Housing (CIH) in response to requests from members. It is intended to assist social housing organisations (that is, housing associations, local authorities and organisations that manage publicly owned housing) to develop, implement and evaluate training programmes for their staff. It is aimed principally at organisations that do not have specialist training staff. It does not deal with professional education to any extent, although appendices do give information on National Vocational Qualifications and Scottish Vocational Qualifications (NVQs/SVQs) and explain the routes to professional qualification. Rather, it focuses on the process of giving people the specific skills, knowledge and attitudes which they need to be effective in their jobs.

The CIH believes that now, as never before, there is a need for social housing organisations to take a strategic approach to the management of training and to have in place systems which will enable them systematically to:

- assess the current and future training needs of the organisation and of the individuals within it
- judge how best to meet those needs, over what time–scale and with what resources
- select appropriate training from the range of possibilities
- plan and evaluate inputs and outcomes
- evaluate and review each phase of planning for training before moving on to the next.

When resources are scarce it is essential that they are used wisely. The Chartered Institute of Housing hopes that this handbook will help organisations to make the best possible use of their resources for training.

1.2　　Structure of this handbook

Each chapter of the handbook discusses and illustrates a different aspect of training management including examples of current good practice. Samples of training documentation drawn from material provided by housing organisations in Britain are provided at the end of each chapter.

A number of devices have been used to help the reader:

- many of the organisations which will use this publication will not have dedicated training staff but will have a particular postholder whose responsibilities include training. For the sake of clarity, throughout this handbook that person is referred to as the Training Officer

- at the end of each chapter there is a piece about Apocryphal Housing Association (AHA). As the name suggests, Apocryphal Housing Association does not really exist but is used to illustrate some of the points made in the chapter. Any resemblance to an existing housing association is purely coincidental!

- throughout the book are examples of good practice drawn from genuine housing organisations. A list of these examples may be found on page iv and notes on the contributors are in appendix 1.

- also throughout the book are boxes in which appear material intended to emphasise or illustrate important points made in the text

- the quotations which appear at intervals in the text, have been contributed by individuals who are not from housing organisations. They are anonymous for obvious reasons!

Following this Introduction, **Chapter 2** describes how to prepare for the systematic management of training. **Chapter 3** discusses the identification of training needs in the context of strategic planning and then **Chapter 4** suggests how needs might be analysed and a training plan devised. **Chapter 5** describes some of the in–house training methods which can provide alternatives to sending people away on courses. **Chapter 6** offers some guidance on the process of training evaluation, monitoring methods and record keeping. Finally, the appendices provide information about: the housing organisations which contributed to this publication; sources of advice and information on training; housing education; and references and further reading.

Chapter 2
Preparing to manage training

2.1   Introduction

There are certain prerequisites for the effective management of training in any organisation. Policy decisions must be made which set a framework for the detailed planning of training and which determine the amount of money to be spent. Then, crucially, someone has to be given responsibility for implementing the policy and managing the budget. This chapter looks at each of these preparative activities in turn.

2.2 Training policies

2.2.1 What are training policies?

They are statements which define the organisation's intentions regarding training. They need not be lengthy or detailed statements but they should be explicit so that everybody in the organisation knows what they can expect and what is expected of them.

Why have a training policy?

A written policy is a useful statement of the [Housing] Association's criteria (and exceptions) for training. It can be a useful reference for administrative points, provide a focus, be used for continuing professional development or a career development programme and as part of the equal opportunities procedure (in order to redress gender or ethnic imbalances), be linked with performance appraisals, improve training needs analysis, co–ordinate the approach by all managers, be useful in training budget control, take account of operational considerations e.g. how many people out on day release, and it can identify different methods of training.

What should be included?

A statement of objectives can be used to introduce the document which could also include references to training needs analysis, in–house and external training, educational courses i.e. which courses will be supported, shadowing/mentoring, job rotation/secondment, booking arrangements, training records and monitoring, budgets, when qualifications lead to salary increments, 'other costs' e.g. excess travel, lunches, excess child–minding, and when costs are to be borne by staff themselves.

From "Training Policies" in *Housing Training News*, No 4, May 1992.

The policies should:

- make clear the value which the housing organisation places on training

- state who is responsible for organising and evaluating training

- state who will receive training and under what circumstances

- define the organisation's priorities

- define the level of available resources, such as the provision of a training budget or a commitment to give every staff member a specified number of days training per year.

2.2.2 Why have training policies?

Training policies are needed for the same reasons as are policies for other areas of management. Training policies are useful because they:

- define expectations, responsibilities and constraints

- provide a framework for the preparation of detailed training plans

- form the basis of the evaluation system. The policy framework can be used to measure the extent to which the training activities are achieving what the organisation intended

- give a clear message to staff about the value which their employing organisation gives to training and how that will be translated into action.

- aid equality of access to training opportunities by defining entitlements and expectations in terms of postholders rather than the particular individuals.

Good Practice Example 1

Notting Hill Housing Group has produced a comprehensive policy document. In their training policy statement they identify these key areas:

* responsibility for training provision
* induction training
* equal opportunities
* the use of in–house courses
* the use of external agencies
* courses of study
* health and safety training
* training for managers
* administration of the training programme.

The policy statements for responsibility for training provision define the specific levels of training responsibility for managers, individual staff members and the central training service for Notting Hill Housing Group.

For example, managers have the primary responsibility for identifying the training and development needs of their staff, and, with support from the Training Manager, for agreeing with their staff the action needed to meet these needs. Individual participation in training is negotiable except for a few compulsory training activities such as induction for new staff, equal opportunities and Health and Safety training.

The training policy states that the training function will be carried out through:

* the analyses of training needs
* the production of a strategy to match needs with the corporate objectives
* the provision of information to meet a range of needs.
* administration, monitoring and evaluation of training activities.

2.2.3 Links with other policies

Training policies for a social housing organisation cannot be developed in isolation but should link up with the organisation's other policies to ensure a coherent approach to organisational development. Particularly relevant are equal opportunities policies and any policies relating to the organisation's current priorities. These links can enhance the success of corporate strategies and increase the potential for consistent service delivery.

Good Practice Example 2

This example is from York City Council's housing training policy. It says, 'the Council believes that training and development of all its employees is a key element in:

- achieving specific corporate objectives, e.g., improving standards of customer orientation, eliminating discrimination in its employment practices and service delivery

- the development of skills in coping positively with change, e.g., the introduction of new methods of working, of new technology, of the demands of CCT

- offering career development and promotion opportunities to employees who have the potential to learn and apply new skills and knowledge in order to fulfil the Council's objectives'.

2.3   Training budgets

Ideally the housing organisation should have a ring–fenced budget specifically for training. The budget should be managed by the person who is responsible for planning, implementing and evaluating the department's or association's training programme. The duty to balance the budget is a strong incentive for careful planning and evaluation! The officer will, therefore, have a direct interest in the most effective use of resources.

2.3.1 Setting the level of the budget

In practice, the current level of expenditure on training in most organisations owes more to historical levels of spending on training and the negotiating ability of training officers than it does to a carefully thought through policy decision! However, money spent on training is a sound investment for the future. The future of any organisation is very largely dependent on the ability and motivation of the people within it and a properly planned training system is essential to personal and professional development. Rather than being last in the queue when budgets are being allocated, training should be given a high priority.

To give some guidance, the Chartered Institute of Housing recommends a training budget set at 2% of the organisation's salary bill. The Local Government Training Board suggests a target per capita expenditure of 1% of the salary bill for local authority housing departments whilst the Confederation of British Industry recommends 5% of salary bills to private sector employers (LGTB, 1990).

If the budget is not set as a per capita rate, someone will have to decide whether the training plan determines the budget or whether what goes into the training plan depends on how much the organisation is willing and able to devote to training.

2.4   The Training Officer

In social housing organisations which are too small to employ specialist training staff, there is usually a designated member of staff who has responsibility for training. This person should have overall responsibility for the organisation's training strategy and for controlling the training budget, even if he or she delegates some of the tasks to other line managers. For the sake of convenience, that individual will be referred to throughout this book as the Training Officer, even though it is recognised that in practice the "training officer" will have a number of other responsibilities as well.

Although the Training Officer may lack the specialist knowledge of a professional trainer, he or she has the very real advantage of being centrally located within the housing organisation. This means that he or she will have a good understanding of the professional requirements of modern housing management, will know the people for whom training is to be provided and will understand how the organisation works.

Two contrasting examples of handling training responsibilities

Notting Hill Housing Group (NHHG) provides 10000 homes in the London area. It employs 400 staff. To service the training needs of an organisation of this size, NHHG set up a dedicated Training Section with four staff members (three full–time equivalents) . The Training Manager identifies needs and works on strategic training issues. A Training Officer implements the training programme. They are supported by 1.5 Administrators. The Training Section carries out some of the training activities or uses external trainers.

Midshire District Council has a rented stock of about 4500 homes. The Housing Management Department employs 78 staff. The primary responsibility for identifying staff training needs, for setting training budgets and for approving staff attendance on courses lies with the two area managers. In addition, the Accommodation Manager has the strategic responsibility for training within the department. This involves liaison with training bodies and identifying corporate training objectives. Most of the housing department's training needs are met by external trainers or courses.

2.4.1 Requirements of the post

The Training Officer must be senior enough to be involved in the organisation's decision making – or at least, to be consulted and kept informed when corporate decisions are made. Otherwise he or she cannot possibly take a strategic view of training needs and the training will fail to form an integral part of the organisation's development.

The Training Officer must be proactive rather than reactive. Some training textbooks refer to the Training Officer as the "change agent", meaning that this is the person whose task it is to bring about the required changes within the organisation. Clearly this is a key role and the Training Officer needs the active support and co–operation of senior management and Committee Members. Assuming that the Training Officer will also have other duties, the active support will need to include participating in some of the tasks, particularly training evaluation.

A prerequisite for the job is, of course, training! It is unfair and unreasonable to expect someone to take on these responsibilities without any preparation and it also gives a negative message about the value which the organisation places on training. The level of responsibility which goes with the post might be recognised by means of a salary increment.

2.5   Introducing Apocryphal Housing Association

Apocryphal Housing Association is a general needs association with a stock of approximately 1,000, a staff of 25 and expansionist ambitions. It has recently taken on a dynamic new Director who has, in turn, created a new and senior post for a Research and Development Manager whose responsibilities include training.

On appointment, the new Research Manager asks her line manager, the Assistant Director, about AHA's training policy and budget. She is told that the policy isn't written down anywhere, although 'everybody knows what it is' and that the training budget consists of what money is left over once everything else has been done.

The Research Manager has come from a larger association which takes training very seriously, so only slightly deterred, she goes away and drafts a paper on training management which she takes the precaution of sending to the Director as well as to the Assistant Director. The paper has the following sub–headings:

1. Review of AHA's training programme over the previous three years.
2. Review of expenditure on training over the previous three years.
3. Recommendations:
3a. Policy
3b. Training procedures
3c. Training records
3d. Training budget.

The report on items 1 and 2 is somewhat sketchy because no records are kept. However, using documents published by other landlords, she is able to draft a training policy statement for AHA, suggest how and why records should be kept and argue the case for a training budget, to be managed by her.

The Director likes the paper but asks her to add a section on determining individual training needs through annual assessments. Backed by the Director, the Research Manager takes the paper to the next meeting of the Management Committee and argues her case.

The main thrust of her argument is that, if AHA is intending to expand and move into contract housing management for Local Authorities, it must ensure that everybody within the Association is prepared. She talks about the need to train Members, managers and staff in the way local authorities manage their stock, the likely implications of CCT and the skills which will be needed within AHA. Knowing the Committee's current concerns, she makes a particular reference to the need for training in tenant consultation, which is still rudimentary in AHA compared with most local authorities.

The Management Committee is convinced and agrees to adopt the policy, with some amendments, and to ask the Finance sub–committee to discuss the provision of a training budget. The Research Manager is asked to draft a specimen training plan to be brought to a future meeting.

However, the Committee has for some time been concerned about its performance on tenant consultation and involvement and feels that developing this should be given priority at present. The Research Manager is asked to undertake an immediate review of the Association's tenant consultation practices with the Director, and report to the next meeting with recommendations.

The Research Manager and Director decide that this is an ideal opportunity to demonstrate to the Committee the link between AHA's strategic development plans and staff training and go away to work on it with that in mind.

All change!

New staff?
They'll need induction training.

New legislation?
Managers need updating.

New performance indicators?
Everyone needs to know what they are and how they are to be achieved.

New computer system?
Operators need training.

New Director/Committee with new policies?
Training throughout the organisation is required to make sure everyone understands and operates the new system.

Reorganisation?
People will not know what to do without training.

Junior manager just got her PD?
Now what training does she need to prepare her for senior management responsibilities?

Local office staff worried about security?
Would a training package which included handling conflict, negotiating skills and self defence make them feel safer?

And when all that is done, things will have changed and it will be necessary to start all over again!

Chapter 3
Identifying training needs

3.1 Introduction

The identification of training needs can be thought of as two distinct, but complementary, processes. On one level the organisation has its own set of personnel training requirements; it must ensure that its staff, managers and Committee members have the knowledge and skills needed to take the organisation forward. At another level, the people within the organisation have their own individual packages of needs which change over time. Both sets of needs must be identified before a plan for meeting some or all of them can be devised.

Above all, relating change to training and training to change are dynamic processes, not a once and for all task easily accomplished on a wet Friday afternoon!

This chapter explains why the identification of training needs is important. It then outlines how to collect information on the needs of the organisation and the individuals within that organisation.

3.2   The Housing Organisation's training needs

Any organisation which is operating in a changing environment needs to have a mechanism for the continuous definition and redefinition of its objectives and strategies. It is becoming increasingly common to have 'business' plans which formalise this strategic planning process and which make clear statements about how the organisation intends to operate over a defined period of time.

No matter how careful the strategic planning process has been, the plans cannot be implemented unless the people who make up the organisation are equipped to play their parts effectively. This means knowing what skills, knowledge and attitudes are currently within the organisation and assessing how these need to be changed in order to realise the organisation's ambitions.

....

Good Practice Example 3

The London Borough of Newham's housing department is one of the pilots for housing management CCT. As part of the process of preparing for this major organisational change, the department has developed a CCT training strategy and planned a comprehensive training programme to assist the process.

The strategy has two aims:

1. to prepare the housing service for CCT

2. to help achieve the Council's ambition of winning contracts put out to tender.

The published training plan has the following columns:

- element
- target group
- issues (to be covered)
- delivery methods
- timescale
- cost.

Training is to be provided for all grades of managers and staff, Housing Committee Members and tenants. Separate training is provided for client–side staff and contract–side staff as appropriate.

The elements include:

- information dissemination
- strategy formulation
- idea exchange
- culture exchange
- business planning
- contract documentation
- tender preparation and evaluation
- contract management
- financial skills
- negotiation skills
- marketing skills
- personnel practices/management
- customer care
- computer systems
- process improvement.

The Housing Training Unit is responsible for planning and implementing the training and for evaluating the strategy.

Good Practice Example 4

Sedgefield District Council offers an interesting example of the use of training to assist major organisational changes.

Specific training objectives were identified prior to the restructuring of three distinct areas of the housing service into a generic local estate management service. Staff who formerly worked in rent recovery, technical and housing management sections needed to acquire new sets of job–specific skills as well as a consistent approach to dealing with the public and working as a team. The spin–off to the process of thinking through the measurable skills for a Local Estate Officer was the contribution to the new job descriptions.

Sedgefield developed a training workbook for each member of staff to complete. Although the workbook was designed to develop a generic competence in the housing staff, the organisation recognised that each staff member would already be technically competent in the skills that related to the section they formerly worked in. Therefore, they could sign off fairly quickly in the areas where they were already skilled and concentrate on the new areas. This meant that staff members were working at a different speeds, but all needed to reach the cut–off date for completion of the training workbook.

Each page of the workbook defined the information needed to complete a task. For example, for the task of effective communication the workbook contained these headings:

Objectives:
To effectively communicate with the public, other departments, colleagues in the Housing Department by phone and in person.

Knowledge required:
Housing legislation, Council policies, structure of the authority.

Time allowed for completion:
3 months

Before the final assessment an interview took place between the employee and at least two senior Managers to assess the Officer's competence in the completed tasks. The contribution to the relevant

Area Team was also assessed on the basis of factors like operating within a team environment, attitude to work and response to dealing with people. The successful completion of the Workbook and the final interview enabled the housing officers to progress to Local Estate Officer posts with management responsibility based on Areas rather than functions.

3.3   Taking the staff with you

Any specific strategic planning objective requires some form of training needs audit. By thinking through the total resource implications, the organisation is much more likely to achieve its goals and maximise the use of its resources. The explicit recognition by senior management that new objectives require a training plan for staff at all levels can ensure that the staff are willing partners in change.

Although this whole process may appear laborious to small organisations operating under pressure, time and effort put in at this early stage may avoid costly and embarrassing repercussions later. It need not be a particularly complicated exercise but it does require someone to be given the authority and time to do it. Of course, when it has been done for the first time an information base has been established which will only need updating rather than re–creating as the business plan changes and staff come and go.

3.4   Identifying the individual's training needs

The identification of the organisation's training requirements is a "top down" approach. This should be done in association with a "bottom up" exercise in which the particular needs of individuals are considered.

An individual's training needs can be assessed on three levels:

• the fit between the needs of the person and the organisation's current and future objectives

- the fit between the individual's skills, knowledge and attitudes and those they actually need for their current and future work

- personal development needs.

Again this is a dynamic process rather than a once and for all statement. An obvious example is that a newly promoted senior housing officer will need training which is tailored to her immediate responsibilities, but in due course her training needs will have evolved into preparation for the next promotion.

One approach is to use the appraisal interview as an opportunity for each staff member to discuss with their line manager what training is needed or wanted. The discussion should centre around the requirements of the post currently held, with the job description acting as a reference point to establish:

- what skills or knowledge does the job require?

- does the person concerned posses them?

Unless there is a complete match between the skills and knowledge required and the skills and knowledge already possessed, there is probably a training need.

The staff member should also be asked to look to the future and suggest training which they would like in order to prepare for promotion, increase professional competence or develop personal skills.

....

Good Practice Example 5

Delyn Borough Council conducted a training audit in the Housing Services Department. Initially, the audit objectives were agreed by the Training Officer, The Head of Housing Services and the Section Heads.

Delyn's Training Officer used the following approach to ensure a good communication loop between the Training Section and the subjects of the audit:

- a staff briefing by the Section Head about the forthcoming audit

- a staff meeting with the Training Officer to discuss the purpose and method of the audit
- completion of individual questionnaires
- collation of Personnel and Training records for all staff taking part in the audit
- detailed examination of job descriptions
- private interviews based on the completed questionnaires
- issue of a report on the Training Audit
- issue of a response to the Training Audit by the Sections.

The training audit looked at these areas of activity:

- induction training
- Health and Safety regulations
- contingencies
- systems and procedures
- customer care
- communication
- management
- training requests.

Specific goals emerged from the assessment of individual training requests. For example, in the Administrative Section, staff requested training in:

- word processing skills
- audio typing
- basic accounting
- letter writing
- coping with aggression.

Generally, among the Administrative staff, the training audit identified two latent training and development issues. One was the desire to increase the level of responsibility and challenge in the posts. The other was the wish to improve skills, so that the staff in the section could broaden their job descriptions.

It is useful to record the information collected on a standard proforma in order to make the eventual analysis of training needs easier. The completed forms are then sent to the responsible officer to an agreed time–scale.

Another way to collect training needs information is to send staff and managers an annual questionnaire on which they are asked to record the training they have had and the training they feel they need, perhaps ticking off a list of topics. The Training Officer has the task of collating the responses and converting the information into a training plan.

Good Practice Example 6

Bradford and Northern Housing Association conduct annual appraisal interviews for all staff members. Staff complete an appraisal form that includes the following questions which they take to an interview with the line manager:

- what do you consider to be the most important duties/key tasks of your present job
- does the job make full use of your capabilities
- what training or practical experience would help you to overcome weaknesses or areas of inexperience?
- indicate the key goals/major objectives to be addressed for the next year
- indicate action proposed for the next 12 months to remedy weaknesses or consolidate strengths and identify any training requirements.

The subsequent interview focuses on the issues raised by the staff member on the form. When specific training objectives are identified, an action plan is agreed, that is then built into the corporate training plan for Bradford and Northern Housing Association.

The example illustrates that the identification of individual training needs involves the perceptions of both the individual staff member and the line manager. Input from both parties at this stage helps the Training Officer with the subsequent task of analysis.

3.5   Training – an opportunity or a threat?

It is important to establish a culture in which everyone in the organisation values training and takes it seriously. Training should be seen as a process of continuous development rather than an ad hoc or sporadic activity and realistic training and development plans will assist this process. This positive attitude will need to be communicated from the very top and the message should be constantly reinforced by example and by training plans which are stimulating and imaginative.

Providing a regular opportunity for all grades of staff (and also committee members where appropriate) to state what training they feel they need or would like is one step towards this goal. However, it should not be allowed to generate unreasonable expectations and everyone should understand that their training and development needs may not be met promptly and fully because there are always resource constraints. A training policy will make it easier for people to understand how and why training will be prioritised.

Managers will also find that some people will feel threatened rather than pleased by the offer of training. This is particularly a risk if information about training needs is collected as part of an annual staff appraisal and it is interpreted as a criticism of performance. Great care will be needed to avoid the implication that managers will send 'inadequate' staff off for remedial training! Clearly, it is vital that managers themselves should be properly trained in conducting this part of the appraisal exercise.

Once the statements of training needs have been collected, people will need some acknowledgement. If staff think that their requests simply fall into a black hole or that the training plans are bureaucratic window–dressing, cynicism will set in very quickly. Ideally, every staff member and manager should be given an individual training plan, but if this is not possible a system for feedback, perhaps via line managers, on what training can be provided and likely time–scales, will help to convince people that they are taken seriously and that the exercise is worthwhile.

....

Good Practice Example 7

Kirklees Metropolitan Borough Council issues three different forms for the self–diagnosis of training and development needs. Managers and non–managers complete forms that focus on educational, vocational and personal development needs.

More unusually, Kirklees also uses the same approach to analyse the needs of senior managers and Chief Officers in relation to specific strategic issues like CCT and Community Care.

The form used for managers encourages the consideration of both the strengths and weaknesses of job performance . For example:

- What are the major difficulties in carrying out your work? Please include personal difficulties.

- Have you any skills, aptitudes or knowledge not fully utilised in your job?

- Is there any special help or 'coaching' you would like from your manager?

- Please list the training programmes you have attended or the additional qualifications you have gained.

- How do you see your career development within Kirklees in the next five years?

....

3.6   Apocryphal Housing Association responds to a changing environment

As requested, the Director and Research Manager go to the Management Committee with a report on tenant involvement. They have concluded that AHA's policies and practices have become outdated and no longer meet the Association's requirements. The Committee decides to accept the recommendations to revise its business plan to give priority to developing tenant participation and accepts the need to include staff training as part of the strategy. The objectives are:

- to have a fully operational tenant consultation system in place within AHA within two years

- to ensure that all staff and managers are given training in those aspects of tenant involvement which are relevant to their present jobs

- to have in place a training plan which will meet the Association's likely future requirements, having particular regard to bidding for housing management contracts.

The Research Manager goes away to put together a detailed plan with proposed targets and time–scales plus an assessment of the costs involved.

She begins by setting out a check–list of questions designed to establish what resources AHA already has and what the training needs are. The check–list includes the following questions:

- what is the current level of in–house expertise in this area?

- how many staff have skills gained through practical experience of working in tenant participation within AHA or elsewhere?

- how many have had formal training?

- who is knowledgeable about relevant legislation, the latest guidance from the National Federation of Housing Associations and the Housing Corporation and sources of funding?

- which posts will require involvement in tenant participation, either as managers or as workers? Exactly what knowledge and skills are required from each postholder?

- what is the attitude of key people towards tenant participation?

- can the people who already have the appropriate skills/knowledge be moved to the posts which will require them?

- what training will be required by the tenants in order to achieve the provisional targets?

- what is the immediate training shortfall? That is, how many people will need to be given how much training before the HA's objective of developing tenant participation to the provisional targets can be implemented?

- allowing for promotion, natural wastage and the staffing demands of the other strategic objectives over the period, what medium to long term training programme will ensure that the HA maintains sufficient numbers of appropriately trained staff?

- would it be better to attempt to meet some of the skills/knowledge requirements by recruiting new staff with relevant experience?

- how can immediate and longer term training needs be met internally?

- what training will have to be bought in?

- what resources are needed in order to meet AHA's provisional targets for tenant participation?

- what resources are available, including any grant aid?

- if there is a shortfall how can it best be met? What would be the impact on the other items in the annual plan?

Having established what she needs to know, the Research Manager begins to collect the information together. One tool she finds particularly useful is the Director's new system of individual training needs assessment. Before the first round of interviews, line managers are briefed to ask all their staff about their level of training and experience in this area of management and to detail the training required by each person in order to meet AHA's objectives.

Once all the information is in place, the Research Manager can put together a comprehensive training plan tailored to the needs of the organisation as a whole and to the individuals within it.

Kirklees Metropolitan Borough Council
Individual Training & Development Needs Analysis

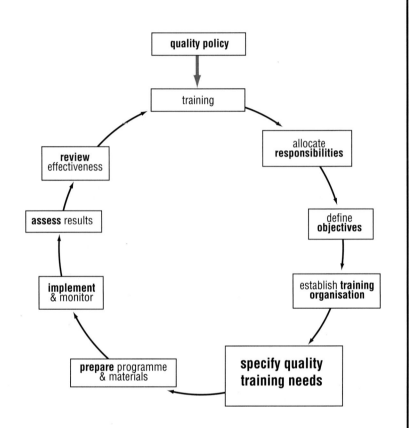

Non-managers at all levels

Introduction

A Training and Development Needs Analysis is a way of finding out your learning and development needs.

What skills and knowledge do you need to do your job competently?

The question can be approached at three levels:

- at an organisational level

- at a job or occupational level

- at an individual level

We will be looking at training needs on an individual level in order to:

- assist managers in looking at the developmental needs of their staff.

- create a way of passing that information to senior managers and to the Training and Development Service to ensure that training and development provided is aimed at your priority needs.

- make the best use of our limited resources by taking action that is relevant and effective.

NB Any written return to the Training and Development Service will not contain identifiable information on individual staff members.

The process for staff

1. With your line manager, **look at the knowledge, skills and behaviour you need to be able to do your job.**

   On the *Skills Assessment Form* we have provided a list of skills to help you do this. If you wish to add to or change this list, please do. It is aimed at stimulating thought and not intended to provide a definitive list of any one personís job.

   You should keep the *Skills Assessment Form* and *Training Record* yourself to use in supervision sessions.

2. Fill out the Learning Action Plan. This helps identify your most important training and development needs and looks at how these

might be met. We suggest you and your line manager keep a copy of this plan.

Your line manager will use information from the *Learning Action Plan* to fill out a *Unit Return* stating your unitís priority training and development needs.

The process for Line Managers

1. Discuss and complete the appropriate *Skills Assessment* and *Training Record* with all members of your staff. Each staff member should keep their forms.

2. Complete a *Learning Action Plan* with each member of staff. Both of you should retain a copy for future use and reference.

3. Complete the *Unit Return* using the information you have gathered. Send it to your line manager with a copy to the Training and Development Service–Personal Services.

4. Complete *Skills Assessment*, *Training Record* and *Learning Action Plan* for yourself with your line manager.

   You will have a contact person in the Training and Development Service for any help or clarification you may need.

Training and Development record

Name:

Unit: Date:

Training and Development – e.g., Courses attended;

Other experiences/skills, or knowledge which helps you do your job better;

Formal educational and work related qualifications (degree, professional qualifications, BTEC, CMS, computer qualifications);

Learning Action Plan

Identifying your Learning Needs

You could either fill in this plan simply using your own view of what skills are needed for the job you do, or, you could use the attached list of skills to help you in this. (see Skills Assessment Form).

Most work related learning and development takes place on the job and not on training courses, so learning activities might include any of the following:

- on–the–job coaching
- off–the–job training course
- planned work experience/delegation
- gathering information/reading, videos etc.
- pairing with other worker
- office based training sessions

When you have filled this form in your line manager will collate your unitís learning needs and send this to the Training and Development Service–Personal Services. It will then be used to plan next yearís training and development programme.

Skill Area	Urgency	Learning activity	Date completed

Training Needs Analysis – Unit Return

Establishment/Unit: _____

Contact person and Tel. No.: _____

1. Priority Training and Development Needs

Now and for next 12 months, in order of priority. Please include all skills/knowledge areas which are essential to you, including those on which we already offer courses.

Course Topic/Skills area	For how many	Degree of urgency *
_____	_____	_____
_____	_____	_____
_____	_____	_____
_____	_____	_____
_____	_____	_____
_____	_____	_____
_____	_____	_____
_____	_____	_____

* Immediate • 0 – 6 months • 6 – 12 months • 12 months plus

2.   Additional Comments on the above

Skills Assessment Form

Use another person to help you assess your competence in these skills, scoring 0 = LOW, 9 = HIGH and selecting a number in that range, e.g., a score of 5 would be moderate. Put the score in the Agreed skill level column.

Use the Importance to job column to rate how important that skill is to the successful performance of your job (Scoring 0 = LOW, 9 = HIGH) and select a number in that range, e.g., a score of 5 would be moderate.

	Personal Skills	Agreed skill level	Importance to job
A	**Self (All Staff)**		
1	Prioritising tasks		
2.	Planning ahead		
3.	Monitoring and evaluating work		
4.	Managing stress		
5.	Identifying development needs		
B	**With Other Staff (All Staff)**		
1.	Team, group & co–working skills		
2.	Working with different professionals /disciplines		
3.	Working within organisational policies		
C	**Communication Skills (All Staff)**		
1.	Reading, writing and interpreting documents		

2.	Working with numbers		
3.	Administrative skills		
4.	Listening and observational skills (including non–verbal communication)		
5.	Ability to build & maintain relationships		
6.	Interviewing techniques		
7.	Counselling skills		
8.	Assertiveness		
9.	Advocacy on behalf of service users		
D	**Staff Working in Social Services**		
1.	Confidentiality		
2.	Clients rights and choices		
3.	Individual beliefs and identifies		
4.	Protecting individuals from abuse		
5.	Loss and change		
6.	Health and safety		
7.	Assessment skills		
8.	Care planning		
9.	Evaluating care		
10.	Managing aggression		
11.	Promoting independence		

12.	Mobility & movement		
13.	Different forms of care		
14.	Mental health		
15.	HIV/AIDS		
16.	Anti–discriminatory practice in terms of:		
	17. Race		
	18. Gender		
	19. Physical disability		
	20. Age		
	21. Religion		
	22. Sexual orientation		
	23. Learning disability		
E	**Staff Working in Housing Services**		
1.	Provide information for clients		
2.	Contribute to administration of contracts for housing		
3.	Contribute to communicating housing policies, programmes and services		
4.	Contribute to the exchange and processing of information		
5.	Plan own work activities		
6.	Maintain an effective working environment		

7.	Provide information and support for clients		
8.	Administer contracts for housing		
9.	Communicate housing policies, programmes and services		
10.	Exchange and process information for decision making		
11.	Organise provision of housing for clients		
12.	Organise repairs and maintenance of housing and other property		
13.	Contribute to the planning and control of budgets and housing finance operations		
14.	Contribute to the planning, organisation and evaluation of work		
15.	Maintain and develop an effective working environment		
16.	Develop and maintain the administration of contracts for housing		
17.	Communicate and promote housing policies, programmes and services		
18.	Contribute to the development of housing policies, programmes and services		
19.	Develop and maintain information exchange and processing		
20.	Manage finance for housing services		
21.	Monitor and evaluate policies, plans and the provision of housing services		

22.	Develop teams, individuals and self to enhance performance	
23.	Plan, allocate and evaluate work carried out by teams, individuals and self	
24.	Create, maintain and develop an effective working environment	
F	**Staff Working in Resource Group**	
1.	Maintain and improve service and product operations	
2.	Contribute to the implementation of change in services, products and systems	
3.	Recommend, monitor and control the use of resources	
4.	Contribute to the recruitment and selection of personnel	
5.	Develop teams, individuals and self to enhance performance	
6.	Plan, allocate and evaluate work carried out by teams, individuals and self	
7.	Create, maintain and develop an effective working environment	
8.	Seek, evaluate and organise information for action	
9.	Exchange information to solve problems and make decisions	

Appendix to skills assessment form

This appendix needs tailoring to your needs.

This can be done by using the *Additional Skills* column to identify skills relevant to your service area. Job descriptions and personnel specifications may assist in this process as well thinking of the job undertaken in the following ways;

Break down the job into the main key responsibility areas
- What knowledge and skills are needed to do the job?
- Has the job changed over the last year, or is it likely to change in the following year?
- If so how?
- What are the personal development implications of these changes?

G	Additional Skills	Agreed skill levels	Importance to job
1			
2			
3			
4			
5			
6			
7			
8			
9			
10			

Priority Training and Development Grid

You may find it useful to use the grid below, with your line manager, to identify your priority training and development needs.

Plot each competence score according to its agreed skill level and its importance to job.

For example, skill A4, you may feel needs development and has an agreed skill level of 2. If it is important for your job, its importance score might be 8. This would appear in the crucial section of the grid.

You can then see at a glance those skills which are crucial to your job and which need swift action!

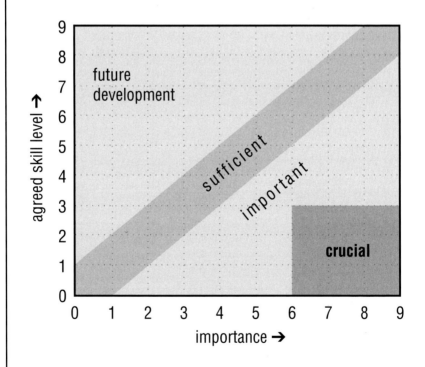

Chapter 4
Analysing needs and devising training plans

4.1   Introduction

Having collected information about the training needs of individuals
and of the organisation as a whole, the Training Officer is faced with the
tasks of analysing the needs and then planning how to meet them. This
phase is critical but need not be as difficult as it might at first seem! The
training policy provides the framework on which to build and the

budget will automatically set limits on expenditure. All that is needed is a systematic approach.

4.2   Reviewing the organisation's training needs

The starting point for this should be the housing organisation's current training policies. For example the training officer will need to know:

- are there any changes or special initiatives planned which will give rise to a training need across the organisation or for a section of it?

- is it policy that all employees will have a set number of training days per year?

- are there corporate training priorities? (These might be specific topics such as preparing for CCT, customer care, race awareness, computer training, or a commitment to give priority to courses leading to housing qualifications)

- is there a rolling programme of induction and continuation training which must be built into a training plan?

- is there to be equal opportunities monitoring of training requests and uptake?

The training policy gives the Training Officer the operational framework. If there are no stated policies, the Officer must know who will make decisions about competing or conflicting needs and what the decision making process is (and how long it will take!).

Good Practice Example 8

Following a workforce survey, Stirling District Council recognised that measures to improve the representation of women, ethnic minorities and disabled people required a 'systematic Council–wide attempt to implement the Equal Opportunities Policy'.

As part of the process, the Council identified some general training initiatives on Equal Opportunities as proof of their commitment to take action to ensure equality of opportunity in employment practices:

- courses on equal opportunities to be conducted for Officers over a two year period. The selection of courses in the first year included recruitment and selection training with an emphasis on good practice techniques to ensure equal opportunities.
- training for women that included career planning and career and family courses
- presentation skills and public speaking for women
- assertiveness training for women
- courses on guidance and career development for handicapped employees.

These training activities were provided across the Council. Each Department studied its requirements in the context of the corporate plan. For example, women outnumbered men by 13 to 1 in the lowest grade in the Housing Department's workforce. Yet, at the Principal Officer level only one out of five posts was filled by a woman. The Housing Department employed 3 disabled workers which reflected the 3% quota recommended in the action plan.

After analysis of these statistics, the Department specified the following measures:

- encouragement for women and disabled employees to attend positive action training courses
- encouragement for Officers to attend "Introduction to Equal Opportunities" training
- briefing for all senior Managers on their department's obligations under the positive action plan.

Stirling's training schemes are a crucial link between the corporate and the Departmental measures for positive action. The equality targets and areas for improvement were identified at the corporate level, but analysis and implementation of appropriate training requirements were conducted at the Departmental level.

4.3   Reviewing the training needs of individuals.

The analysis of the information collected will usually generate further questions for the Training Officer to answer. These might include:

- what has the assessment of training needs of individual staff/managers revealed? Who wants what and with what degree of urgency? Are there any priority requests?

- are there any patterns or clusters? For example, is there a common need which could be met by providing training across the organisation? Is there any marked trend for people from one section of the department/association to request more or less training than the others? What is the reason for this imbalance?

All this information needs to be recorded and set out in a fashion which makes analysis as easy as possible. Using forms to collect the information in the first place will assist the process but the information then has to be collated. Ideally this process would be computerised, with the Training Officer using a personal computer and dedicated software to record and sort the data. However, if that is not possible, specially designed forms will speed the process.

It is important to keep individual training records that record both the training requested and training completed.

4.4   How does the training budget stand?

At this point the Training Officer will need to know the following:

- what is the total sum of money available? (or is the budget negotiable once the plan is drafted?)
- has a portion of the budget already been earmarked for a particular training initiative?
- should a portion of it be set aside for a particular purpose?
- should all the money be committed at the beginning of the training year or should there be a contingency sum for dealing with unanticipated requirements?

- are there any anticipated staff changes or organisational changes during the year which will create a training need and for which resources should be earmarked?
- is it policy to give each section an equal share of the budget or can spending be skewed?

The Training Officer might have the authority to make the necessary decisions in the absence of a detailed policy statement. If that is not the case, the Training Officer must know how to get these important questions answered.

4.5   Selecting methods of training delivery

Some organisations will be able to call on a specialist Training Department for advice, materials and even trainers to assist with this part of the process. Others may well be able to draw on a similar resource which is regionally or centrally based. But in a great many organisations the Training Officer will have to make the decisions and co–ordinate the programmes alone.

The Training Officer will find it useful to keep a register of training resources. This will include a list of training materials already held within the organisation (books, videos, training packages etc.) and a contact list of individual trainers and organisations which run training courses. In particular the Training Officer will wish to keep a record of the courses run by the Institute of Housing and the National Federation of Housing Associations. Some housing organisations find it useful to join forces to provide training – this is always a path worth considering.

4.5.1 Choosing types of training

"As a fairly new trainer I saw the three day residential course at a top London hotel as a real treat and it never occurred to me that the people on the course would not see it in the same way. But on the first morning, in the lift on the way up to the training room, I overheard some women who were obviously coming to my course talking about how nervous they were about being somewhere so unfamiliar and how they were worried that if they didn't do well

on the course they would lose their jobs. I knew that at least the first day would be lost whilst I gained their trust and built up their confidence."

Since every person has a unique learning style, it makes sense to vary the methods of training delivery. There is a bewildering variety of training resources available, ranging from the high–tech, multi–media, interactive packages to the low–tech book!

Certainly training no longer automatically means "going on a course" and an imaginative approach to providing forms of training can have a number of benefits. Firstly, there is an equal opportunities aspect. People with family commitments or who have a physical disability, often find it particularly difficult to stay away from home or to travel to another venue. Going away to a strange environment with unfamiliar people can also put undue strain on people who lack confidence. Providing alternatives can open up training opportunities to people who would otherwise be excluded or unable to get the full benefit. Secondly, sending people away for courses or conferences, even if they are non–residential, is expensive, and using a training package in–house might be better value in some cases. Thirdly, variety is the spice of life! Varying the training methods will add interest to the training plan and to the training process.

4.6   Drawing up the Training Plan

By this stage the Training Officer has a clear picture of organisational and individual needs and of all the resources available to meet those needs. There is unlikely to be a perfect match!

The first stage in drawing up a training plan for the organisation is to decide which needs can be met in the course of the plan, which cannot be met immediately and which will not be met at all. There will have to be trade–offs between the needs of individuals and the needs of the whole organisation. It will also be necessary to assess the competing needs of individuals or of Sections. Again, the Training Officer will need clear senior management guidance on these decisions, or the authority to make them alone to previously agreed criteria.

Inevitably, some decisions will be very unpopular, but will be more acceptable if they are made within a public and equitable policy framework.

Having made those decisions, the Training Officer can draft the detailed plan. A training plan is simply a costed scheme for implementing the organisation's training policy over a defined period, perhaps one year. Usually it will detail:

- what training is to be provided
- who is to receive that training
- when it will take place
- who is responsible for organising it
- how much it will cost.

What costs should go into the training plan?

- the cost of providing cover for staff who are away on training
- course fees, conference fees
- travelling, accommodation and other subsistence expenses for people attending events away from base
- fees and expenses for trainers or speakers
- purchase or hire of training materials (films, training packages, books, handouts, etc)
- the hire of venues for training, with perhaps an extra element for providing refreshments for those attending
- purchase or hire of training equipment for in–house training (overhead projectors, screens, video cameras, slide projectors, etc).

Each piece of training requires a budget sheet with the expenditure broken down by category and then totalled. It is also helpful to include the number of trainees attending and a calculation of the cost per trainee

---

If feasible at this stage, it is useful to append details of the courses or internal training arrangements, giving dates, times, venues, names of trainers, etc. It is also good practice to outline the objectives of each piece of training and how it is to be evaluated. For events planned for later in the year, it might not be possible to do this immediately but should be put into the diary as a task for later so that it is not overlooked.

When planning dates, thought should be given to:

- the usual peaks and troughs of the organisation's work
- annual leave periods
- any particular events already in the diary which might have an effect on workloads.

As far as possible the plan should avoid increasing the load on sections or individuals by withdrawing people from everyday work at particularly busy periods. As it might seem that there are no periods which are not particularly busy, the Training Officer should be prepared to be imaginative about training methods which achieve their objectives without causing unnecessary disruption!

Some 'time savers' worth considering in your plan

- training staff together who already know each other and get on well together can reduce time spent on introductions

- staff acclimatised to training can learn a great deal in two to four hours rather than a full day session

- training at the place of work, or close at hand (but without telephone or other means of contact!) reduces travel time

- briefing prior to and de–briefing after an event means participants are ready to start, and can capitalise on learning back at the workplace

- it might be possible to close early or open late to accommodate regular staff training or briefing sessions

- some organisations work on 50% cover for regular half–day training slots

---

• others organise well–attended lunchtime sessions

From: *Making Housing Work – with good training*, Local Government Training Board, 1990.

4.6.1 Individual training plans

Ideally each person in the organisation should have an individual training plan, perhaps projected over a longer period of time than the organisation's plan. This would plan and record the person's acquisition of skills and knowledge, including targets where appropriate.

The responsibility for drawing up and maintaining that plan would rest with the individual, but with the advice and assistance of her/his line manager and the Training Officer.

....

Good Practice Example 9

Kirklees Metropolitan Council emphasises its commitment to the development of both the individual and the organisation in its strategy for Employee Development. The Council states that, '...the [training and development] strategy will identify individuals' training needs from induction to skills development. It will aid managers to enable their staff and allow individuals to develop within the organisation'.

Each employee, whether managerial or non–managerial staff, completes an individual form during the annual Training Needs Analysis (TNA) review. The Service Manager and the employee discuss the information on the TNA form in a formal meeting. They then agree a provisional set of training and development objectives for the following twelve months.

Training and Development Services then use this information to develop training plans in collaboration with the Service Managers, 'for all levels of staff to enable the delivery of high quality housing services.'

Depending on the nature of the training and development need, the individual programme could include a mixture of:

- professional courses ranging from BTEC National Certificates to post–graduate qualifications in Housing Studies.

- development programmes to enhance core competencies

- or, appropriate post–qualifying/post–entry learning opportunities.

4.7   Launching the training plan

In an organisation already familiar with the annual round of planing for training or in a culture which perceives training as an opportunity rather than a threat or a bore, there will be little or no need to "sell" the plan. However, in most cases there will be at least some people who will want to challenge certain decisions, ask for amendments or who are unable to attend certain events.

It is therefore a sensible precaution for the Training Officer to issue the plan in draft for comment before finalising it. The plan, or the relevant parts of it, should be circulated to everybody with an interest, including Committee Members, and time allowed for comments and necessary revision.

Junior staff should have a chance to express an opinion on training programmes which involve them. In order to ensure commitment and a good take–up rate for courses and training events, all staff will need to feel comfortable with the timetable and method of delivery. A reluctant or stressed trainee is unlikely to get much benefit from a course, however well planned and conducted.

However irksome this stage may seem to the Training Officer who will almost certainly have many other things to do, it is important that the training plan should be 'owned' by the whole organisation. Otherwise, a great deal of effort can be wasted as a result of people lacking commitment to the activities planned.

Once agreed, the plan should be issued and distributed as widely as possible. Amendments during the life of the plan are inevitable and the Training Officer should negotiate and publish updates on new or changed events as required, ensuring that everyone in the organisation is kept in the know.

4.8 Apocryphal Housing Association – Outline Training Plan for Tenant Consultation

The Research Manager has begun to draw up a draft training plan for implementing the tenant consultation strategy drawing on the analyses of organisational and individual training needs. She sets out the following framework:

1. **Objectives:** fully operational tenant consultation system to be in place by end December 1995; all staff to be trained for responsibilities in present posts; training programme to meet future Association requirements.
2. **Time–scale of this plan:** detailed plan for 1994, outline plans for 1995 and 1996.

3. No. of Staff and Committee members included in this plan: all.

Note: there is also a requirement for tenant training. This is covered in a separate, but complementary, plan.

4. **Budget:** £5,000 allocated for year one. £2,000 provisionally allocated for each of years 2 and 3.

5. **Training events in Year 1:**

   5(a) **Introductory training** to cover the reasons for tenant involvement, legal requirements, possible structures and good practice elsewhere.
   For: all staff and committee members
   Method: seminars with presentations by Director
   Location: in–house

   5(b) **AHA's new policies and procedures**
   For: all staff and committee members

Method: series of workshops led by Research Manager
Location: in–house

5(c)   **Handling meetings:** presentation skills, assertiveness training, agenda and minute writing, chairing meetings, report writing.
For: Area Managers, then staff who will work directly with tenants' groups and representatives
Method: workshops led by external trainer then trickle training by managers to staff
Location: in–house

5(d)   **Forms of tenant management:** Tenant Management Committees, Tenant Co–ops, Tenant Management Organisations, Residents' Democracy, Estate Management Boards and other tenant management initiatives.
For: Interested committee members and all managers
Method: six weekly training sessions conducted by external trainer
Location: in–house

5(e)   **Developing Tenant Involvement In Housing Associations**
For: interested committee members, managers and staff
Method: one day course run by Eastshire HA Training Consortium
Location: external (venue to be announced)

For each of the planned events the Research Manager lists the postholders who need to attend (first priority) and then those individuals, not on the first list, who would like to attend (second priority). Then she works out a cost for each event, remembering to include items like the cost of handouts and the trainers' travelling and fee costs. All these are entered onto the plan and the total checked against the budget. Next she enters provisional dates. Finally, the Research Manager has to plan the evaluation methods for each method of training. Then the draft plan for year one is ready for circulation.

Once everyone has had a chance to comment, the Research Manager amends the plan as required and moves on to the implementation, monitoring, evaluation and review stages. In the mean time she is working on the outline plans for years two and three.

Good Practice Example 10

Notting Hill Housing Group publishes a training programme for events held at its own training centre. They also circulate details of other events separately. A sample from the Notting Hill course programme gives this information:

Communicating assertively for women
Two day course
Date: 13 and 14 February
Time: 9:45 am – 5:00 pm
Venue: NHHG Training Centre

Target group:

Women who would like to improve their communication in the workplace and would like to explore how the principles of assertive behaviour could help.

Course objectives:

* to gain an understanding of the basic principles of assertion
* to review responses to difficult behaviour from others
* to formulate an action plan to manage change in communicating assertively in the workplace.

Kirlees Metropolitan Borough Council
Housing Training Plan 1992/93   April 1992

1.   Introduction

1.1   This document sets out the Servicesí main aims and objectives for workforce training for the financial year 1992/93.

1.2   The training programme delivered by the Training Section is published through the Calendars, the Course Programme Booklets all of these are distributed widely throughout the service.

1.3   The training service is limited by the human, financial and technical resources allocated to the function, and our aim to maximise provision within these restraints.

2.   Commitment to Training

2.1   The overall purpose of the training service is to assist and encourage all staff to acquire skills and knowledge to the standard needed to meet the service objectives and service standards.

2.2   Training Plan

The training plan for the Training Section is underpinned by the following statement of purpose:-

• to provide quality training for staff in the Personal Services Group including support staff on qualifying courses.

• to develop, maintain and make available training resources to staff within the Personal Services Group.

- to maintain records of training and budget expenditure.

2.3   Equal Opportunities

The training service is committed to the Councilís statement on equal opportunities, which is attached as Appendix 1.

2.4   This statement is taken seriously by the training service and courses will be regularly reviewed to ensure that equality issues are reflected both in the content of the course, and the conditions under which the course is presented. We expect our training staff to challenge behaviour which is inappropriate to equality of opportunity.

2.5   This section contains budgetary considerations.

3.   *Current Issues*

3.1   The Children Act and the Community Care Act, will effect housing allocations and service delivery.

3.2   The training service needs to be ready to support staff as they prepare for Service Planning and Review, Tenants Charter and training systems interventions via information technology (repairs, allocations and rents) as well as the possible effects of Compulsory Competitive Tending.

3.3   The other major issue is the implementation of NVQ framework on the provision of Housing and Personal Services Training. This could fundamentally affect the organisation of the force in the training service and affect the training out–puts as well as the allocation of budgets.

3.4   This year staff are working with a pending restructure. This contributes to an atmosphere of uncertainty.

3.5   The Councilís initiatives of providing Quality Services, Customer Care and the Anti–Poverty Strategy will also underlay the training from our section.

4.   *Strategy*

4.1   A panel has been in place for some time to make decisions as to which applications for professional courses are accepted.

4.2   The panel may well be merged into the mirror group of the Employee Development Strategy Group as the Personal Services Group achieves greater cohesion.

4.3   The Arcast Personnel System will soon be up and running. This will enable us to, establish and maintain training records from a workforce list.

4.4   The existing Training Needs Analysis, feedback from Service Managers at their Away Day in March 1992 and diagnostic questionnaire with Senior Managers formed the basis of our training plans for this year.

4.5   During this year the existing Training Needs Analysis form will be reviewed and it is proposed to develop a new Training Needs Analysis which is linked to competencies and staff development in a more objective way.

Kirklees Metropolitan Borough Council
Equal Opportunities Policy Statement

1.   The Policy

Kirklees Metropolitan Borough Council is committed to providing services and employment opportunities on an equitable basis to all. The aim of the Equal Opportunities Policy is to ensure that users of Council services and present and potential employees do not receive less favourable treatment on the basis of sex, marital status, disability, sexual orientation, race, colour, nationality, ethnic origin, religious belief, age, trade union, political activity or, through any other unjustifiable cause.

The Council is committed to positive action and is introducing changes which are necessary to make the policy effective. A central Equal Opportunities Unit, in conjunction with specialist directorate based equal opportunities officers, has been established in order to initiate, co–ordinate and monitor equal opportunities policies. The result of monitoring will be reported to the Policy and Resources (Equal Opportunities/Equal Rights) Sub–Committee. Training will be provided to promote non–discriminatory recruitment and employment practice and, to eradicate all forms of racism, sexism and negative perceptions of disability.

2.   Implementation

The Codes of Employment Practice issued by the Commission for Racial Equality, the Equal Opportunities Commission and Manpower Services Commission will be used as a starting point for the implementation of equal opportunities measures. Codes specific to Kirklees will be developed to establish positive action procedures relevant to local needs. Programmes of action for implementation of the Policy in the delivery of services will also be produced and monitored within service directorates.

3.   *Issuing The Policy Statement*

The statement is being issued to ensure that all employees are aware of the Council's Equal Opportunities Policy and the steps being taken by the Council to monitor and review it. It is vital that all individuals who are employed by the Authority appreciate that they have a responsibility and a role to play in the promotion of equal opportunities. This is particularly so in the day to day relationships which are developed at work between employees and, between employees and users of Council services. The support and co–operation of each employee for the measures now being adopted by the Council is essential to the elimination of discrimination against all sectors of both the work and wider community. The Policy Statement has the full support of the Kirklees Trade Unions.

Equal Opportunities Unit,
Office of the Chief Executive
July, 1986

Personnel Services Group
York City Council
QED: Quality Employee Development

In response to the Staff Survey we have changed the way in which
internal training is organised. A key feature of the new scheme is the
grouping of training modules to form 4 distinct training programmes:

A Supervisory and Management,
B Induction and Re–Entry,
C Customer Care,
D Women into Management.

A *Supervisory and Management*

This programme is for people who are currently supervisors or
managers, or who are hoping to move into such jobs.

A1 The core modules listed on the attached nomination form
represent the essential skills identified by the Management
Charter Initiative as crucial to any manager.

A2 If you take all the core modules plus at least two optional
modules you will be awarded a certificate of attendance for the
Programme.

A3 If you want to achieve this award tick the box on the form at
section A where it states ìI wish to take this whole Programme
for my certificateî and you will automatically be nominated for
all the core modules. You will then have to add your selection of
2 or more optional modules to complete the requirement.

A4 If you have already taken a core module within the last 2 years,
give the details in section E on the form. You will be credited
with this and may be required to take a half–day refresher
instead of the full module.

B *Induction and Re–Entry*

This Programme is for people who are new to York City Council or are returning after a period away from their job (e.g. on maternity leave or long term sickness absence)

B1   There is no Certificate available for this Programme. Just fill in your selection in section B on the application form.

C *Customer Care*

This Programme is for people with front–line or internal customer contact.

C1   If you take all the core modules you will be awarded a certificate of attendance for the Programme.

C2   If you want to achieve this award tick the box on the form at section C where it states ìI wish to take this whole Programme for my certificateî and you will automatically be nominated for all the core modules.

C3   You may also select some optional modules as appropriate to your job. These are not compulsory for a certificate.

C4   If you have already taken a core module within the last 2 years, give the details in section E on the form. You will be credited with this and may be required to take a half–day refresher instead of the full module.

D *Women Into Management*

Despite making up half our workforce, women are under–represented above Scale 6 at York City Council. This programme is for women who feel they are either not achieving their potential and may want to progress into management or are in management posts but want to review their position.

D1   There is no Certificate available for this Programme. Just fill in your selection in section D on the application form.

- Training modules will be held throughout the year and it may take you more than a year to complete a Programme. This is therefore a long–term commitment.

- However, you do not have to take the full programmes. You can opt to take one or two modules instead if you wish. These will be credited to you and you may complete the programme sometime in the future if you want to.

- Courses are not all going to be held over one or two standard days. We hope this will enable more part–time and job share people to attend.

- You can attend any modules regardless of your scale or job.

To apply for a place on any of the modules or programmes:

1. Decide which modules or programmes you would like to apply for. To get further information on these look at the **QED Booklet** held by your departmental training representative or your departmental administrator.

2. OR Come to a 'Training Roadshow' where people will be on hand to explain the new system and give details of the courses on offer. These are being held as part of training hour, lunchtime or team meetings and will be publicised in your department.

3. Fill in the attached form. Please make sure you include your National Insurance Number. This may seem unusual but will enable us to create a unique record for you on our computer database. Your National Insurance number is shown on your pay slip and on the address label on this sheet.

4. Discuss your application with your manager or supervisor and ask them to sign the form at section G to agree their support for your training. They may at this point ask you to modify your application. If you are not happy about this please raise the matter initially with your Chief Officer, then if you are still not satisfied please refer to Personnel.

5. Send your completed form to the Guildhall by 8 May.

6. We will allocate you to specific courses and then notify your manager of the dates of the training in order that they can ensure service cover.

7. When they have agreed the dates with us we will then send you an individual training plan listing all the modules you have opted to take along with details of dates and venues. You should receive this by mid July.

8. If we are unable to meet demand for courses we will put you on a reserve list.

9. Around 6 weeks before each module you will be sent a reminder together with details of any pre–course work.

10. Even if you do not want to take any of these courses please feel free to add your comments in section F of the form and return it to us in order that we may be able to address your training needs in future.

Personnel Services Group
QED Application

National Insurance No.   Surname: First Name:

Dept: Section: Manager/Supervisor:

Sex: M F (please circle one)   Your work phone number/extn:

Grade: (please indicate by ticking in relevant box below)
Scale 1–3 ☐   Scale 4–6 ☐   SO1–2 ☐   Principal Officer ☐   Chief Officer ☐
Manual/Craft ☐

Do you work: Full–time ☐   Part–time ☐   Job Share ☐   Temp Contract*☐
(please tick)   *When does this end?

A) Supervisory and Management Programme
☐   I wish to take this whole Programme for my Certificate (see note A3)

Core Modules
☐   Getting the Right Person for the Job
    (11/2 days + 1 day)
☐   Disability Awareness (1 day)
☐   Employee Relations (11/2 days + 1
    day)
☐   Taking Control of Your Time
    (5 hours)
☐   Managing Customer Care (1 day)
☐   Managing Health & Safety
    (2 x 1/2 days)
☐   Writing Plain English (2 x 1/2 days)
☐   Managing & Motivating Your Team
    (2 x 1 day)
☐   Project Planning (1 day)
☐   Demystifying Local Government
    Finance [General Overview]
    (2 x 1/2 days)

Optional Modules
☐   How YCC makes its decisions
    (1/2 day)
☐   Office Safety (3 hours)
☐   Communicating Positively! (1/2 day)
☐   Handling the Media (1 day)
☐   Assertiveness & You (Men – 2 days)
☐   Assertiveness & You (Women – 2
    days)
☐   Understanding Stress (1 day)
☐   Controlling the Safety of Contractors
    (1 day)
☐   Effective Report Writing (1 day)
☐   Presenting to a Group (11/2 days)
☐   Problem Solving (1 day)
☐   Safe Lifting & Handling (3 hours)
☐   Preparing & Monitoring Budgets
    (1/2 day)
☐   Demystifying Local Government
    Finance [In–depth view]
    (2 x 1/2 days)
☐   Making Meetings Work (1/2 day)

B) Induction and Re–Entry Programme
- ☐ Introduction to York City Council (2 x 1 day)
- ☐ Safe Lifting and Handling (3 hours)

or
- ☐ York City Council from the Inside (1/2 day)

or
- ☐ Welcome Back (1/2 day)

C) Customer Care Programme
- ☐ I wish to take this whole Programme for my Certificate (see note C2)

Core Modules
- ☐ Disability Awareness (1 day)
- ☐ Coping with Aggression (1 day)
- ☐ Professional Customer Care (1 day)
- ☐ Emergency Aid (4 hours)

Optional Modules
- ☐ Effective Use of your Phone (1/2 day)
- ☐ Developing Your Writing Skills (2 x 1/2 days)
- ☐ Office Safety (3 hours)

D) Women Into Management Programme
Select **Either** modules from left **Or** right hand sides.

Either
- ☐ Women Into Management (2 x 3 days)

or
- ☐ Women In Management (2 days)

Or
- ☐ Assertiveness and You – Women (2 days)
- ☐ Taking the Next Step (1 day)

E) Core Modules You Have Taken Within the Past 2 Years

Course Title	Date taken

F) Comments/Feedback
Please state if there are any more areas you would like in–house training to cover?

G) Manager/Supervisor's Agreement Obtained
I have discussed this application with the individual and agree to release them for this training.

Signed: Name: Date

_____   _____   _____

Chapter 5
Learning and teaching in-house

5.1   Introduction

Sending people away on courses and conferences is expensive. Although external training has its uses, there are also many possibilities for providing training to people in-house. This chapter looks at some of those possibilities, beginning with a brief consideration of how people learn.

5.2   Factors which affect learning

There are certain well known factors which have an impact on people's learning and Training Officers will probably find it helpful to be aware of them when designing training plans.

The main points to be considered are:

- the trainee must want to learn. Self motivation is important but the occasional carrot can help! Different 'carrots' will appeal to different people. Some will respond to recognition, others to a chance of promotion or financial reward

- the trainee must consider the subject matter to be important

- it is a good idea to set the trainee a target, that is, a clearly defined standard of acceptable performance. The target must be achievable, but not without effort. It is also necessary to give feedback on progress and to provide help and encouragement when necessary, even if the trainee appears to be highly self–motivated

- the suitability of the training method, the personality of the trainer, the level of complexity and the pace of learning for the individual under training. For the most effective learning, all these need to be as close as possible to ideal for the individual being trained

- the extent to which the learning is subsequently reinforced. No matter how much the trainee has learned, much of it will be forgotten quickly unless it is constantly practised in the work place. This will almost always require an input from the line manager.

If all of those are right, the trainee will be able to derive maximum benefit from the training and so, too, will the organisation.

Careful preparation by the manager or Training Officer is important. The manager should discuss the training with the trainee, establishing with him/her exactly what is needed and why. The trainee will be the best person to judge whether what is planned will help her/him to learn.

The manager or Training Officer will need to monitor progress during the training process and set aside time to evaluate it with the trainee and, if applicable, the trainer, at the end. It is then the manager's responsibility to ensure that the trainee gets sufficient reinforcement of the material learned.

Notes for managers on setting targets for the trainee:

- define the outcome and standard required in clear, unambiguous terms

- decide on the means of determining whether the target has been achieved

- state any conditions which apply

- have a plan in mind for responding to a failure to achieve targets

- also consider how to respond to performance far in excess of targets.

5.3   On–the–job training

This is probably the most commonly used form of in–house training because there are clearly advantages to providing training to someone whilst they continue with their job. It is a training technique which is particularly useful for a staff member who is new to the post and for the practising of skills and techniques learnt theoretically elsewhere.

The main advantages are:

- the trainee is dealing with the realities of the working environment, not a simulation

- it is a low cost training method, usually requiring one or more of the employee's colleagues to give information with no special facilities or materials required

- the content, pace and style of the training can be tailored to the particular needs of the individual

- the timing of the training can be flexible to allow for other commitments and to avoid taking staff out of action at a busy time of the day or week

- there will be an element of team development when the trainee learns from his/her colleagues

- it is relatively easy for the manager to oversee and evaluate.

- it can readily be combined or supplemented with other in–house and external training to meet particular needs.

There are also, of course, some disadvantages:

- the person or people doing the training might not be very good at it!

- the 'trainers' could be passing on bad habits as well as good

- it can be difficult to set the required amount of time aside and keep it free of interruptions

- the trainee, especially if new and inexperienced, might feel nervous about asking questions which might be thought 'silly'

- it is hard to cost this form of training.

There are three basic types of on–the–job training, classified according to who is the active trainer. These are:

- training planned and conducted by the employee's manager

- training carried out by more experienced colleagues

- active learning by the employee.

On–the–job training will rarely be delivered by professional trainers. The following notes on learning and training methods might be helpful to all concerned.

5.3.1 On–the–job training methods

There are a number of possible ways to deliver on–the–job training:

- one–to–one training on a particular skill or process e.g. using a word processor (this may also be done in–house but by taking the trainee away from their desk)

- coaching is a systematic development of the trainee's ability, e.g. developing report writing skills. The manager will plan a series of tasks to be done in the work situation which will gradually build up the employee's ability to write reports in the style required by the organisation. As each task is completed the manager and employee will meet to discuss performance

- job rotation, where a number of staff experience each others' work for a limited period of time

- secondment to another department or organisation can broaden the employee's knowledge and experience, provide a real challenge and help her/him to build links within or between organisations. It is most effective if the secondee is given a specific project in the host organisation so that learning is active and focused

- mentoring is a process whereby an employee is "taken under the wing" of someone more experienced and encouraged to use the mentor for advice, information and support. It can only work if there is no line management between the two parties, otherwise the trainee will not feel able to speak frankly about problems and failures

- discovery learning, or learning by doing, is a useful way of giving the trainee an active role in the training process. The trainee needs to be given a particular task to perform and then have an opportunity to discuss what s/he has learned and to ask questions.

The choice of training method will depend on three main factors: the personality and training needs of the individual trainee; the availability of suitable 'trainers'; the nature of the material to be learned. Monitoring and evaluation will tell the manager whether the chosen method was indeed the correct one. The best question to ask is simply, "does it work?" If it does, then it was the right decision. If it doesn't then another method or another trainer should be tried. Do remember that inexperienced and unqualified trainers will probably need some help.

> *"I was in my first week as a training officer and I was asked to arrange some in–house training with a particular person acting as the trainer. What I didn't know at the time was that she had never done any training before. We both turned up on the morning with all the people who had been sent on the course. Then we discovered that neither of us had thought to organise paper, pencils, flip charts or even coffee! I was terribly embarrassed but I never made that mistake again!"*

....

Good Practice Example 11

Key Housing Association used the results of a training needs analysis when designing its comprehensive in–house training programme. The HA's projects are geographically spread and a range of training methods and materials are used, including a distance learning pack and training events at the HA's Glasgow headquarters or at regional centres.

Key HA's clients have learning difficulties and the HA gives particular importance to induction training for teams going into new projects and for new staff joining existing teams. Whole team induction lasts for two weeks prior to tenants moving into a new scheme and brings staff together to give them an introduction to the values, practices and procedures of the HA, whilst facilitating team building.

New staff joining existing teams are trained over a period of 12 weeks by means of a Key–specific distance learning pack. Support is provided by the line manager and the new staff member is guided through two week modules with objectives and a review period for each module. The induction centres on the procedures handbook and local projects manual and is designed to set the staff member's *"work with tenants in the context of Key's values and practices."*

The training needs of existing staff members are identified through supervision and will be affected by the current support needs of tenants and prevailing local circumstances. The training programme runs from

September to July each year, offering a range of courses. Topics include:

- understanding behaviour which challenges our service
- assertiveness
- sexuality and people with a learning difficulty
- selection interviewing
- towards effective supervision
- report writing
- managing stress
- working with families

Many of the training activities use a mixture of group discussions, case studies, group exercises, lectures and hand–outs to deliver the content of the course. On completion of a section of training, the participants complete a review sheet and discuss the outcomes of the specific courses with a supervisor.

5.4　Other In–House training methods

5.4.1 Short courses

These can be run as an alternative or supplement to sending people out of the organisation on courses and can use either in–house expertise or trainers who have been brought in. Some organisations find it useful to offset some of their expenses by offering places to the staff of neighbouring organisations when the subject matter is of wider interest. This has the further benefit of enabling staff to share experience and develop professional networks with their counterparts in other local organisations.

5.4.2 Quality circles

Quality circles are where training and organisational performance interact most directly. A quality circle is the name given to a group of colleagues who meet to discuss the problems and issues at work which interfere with providing the best possible service to their customers. The emphasis is very much on diagnosing problems and proposing workable solutions, not on having a good moan!

The circle should consist of volunteers and should meet on a regular basis, say once a month. It is important that the comments and suggestions of all group members are treated as being of equal value, regardless of the post held. The circle is led by someone who is able to make this happen and who is in a position to take the circle's proposals forward. The circle leader is then also responsible for giving the members feedback on the progress of their ideas and comments. If the leader is the line manager, he or she will sometimes be able to consider an idea and make a decision on the spot.

Quality circles are worth considering as part of a training plan because, properly run, they can aid the personal development of participants and encourage the growth of managerial skills as well as having a direct benefit on the performance of the organisation. Usually, there will also be a team building aspect.

> *"They set up Quality Circles supposedly to get us all involved in improving our service. Pretty soon we found that people were not being released from work to come to the meetings and word got around that the managers didn't like being criticised. All the Circles have petered out now."*

5.4.3 Regular team or section meetings

Many housing organisations provide training through regular meetings for staff or groups of staff. These can be formal or informal, voluntary or compulsory, with or without outside speakers. The possibilities are endless because all that matters is that it suits the organisation concerned.

Here are some examples from social housing organisations:

- a weekly team meeting for area office staff. The office opens later than usual and all staff are expected to attend. The agenda always includes a training session on some aspect of the job, the topic being chosen by a team member. Sometimes a team member prepares a short presentation for the others

- a weekly lunch club open to all Council staff, not only housing people. There is a speaker on a topic related to local government in general or to this Authority in particular. Recent topics have included quality, local government reorganisation, and CCT

- monthly sessions for wardens. They are partly social because the wardens rarely meet otherwise, but every month a trainer comes to do a session on say, assertiveness or stress management

- a two night residential training session every six months for the senior management team. The time is used partly for strategic planning for the organisation and partly for training on specific management skills.

5.4.4 Guided reading

This is a particularly useful way of teaching an employee any written material, such as the organisation's policies and procedures. The reading does need to be structured and the trainee's progress assessed. The material learned will quickly be forgotten unless it is reinforced by use on the job.

5.4.5 Cascade Training

This is an economical method of delivering training which, when well handled, also has the effect of promoting the development of individuals and of teams within the organisation.

Cascade training simply means training a small number of key people in a particular topic and then those people in turn train others. The second tier of trainees can then train a third tier, and so on. The individuals who are to act as trainers must be carefully selected and prepared but this can be an ideal opportunity to develop the confidence and communication skills of a number of people within the organisation.

Thus, cascade training can have a training effect over and above the primary topic.

Cascade training does need careful monitoring. It can enable the very rapid replication of misunderstanding, unfortunate attitudes or careless errors throughout the organisation! The Training Officer, or another manager with a particular interest or expertise, should make periodic checks on the quality of the training and on the quality of the learning.

5.4.6 Distance learning

Distance, or correspondence, learning is another training method particularly useful for people who want to study whilst continuing with their job. Appendix 3 lists some of the organisations which provide distance learning courses specifically for housing managers. The Open University and other colleges and universities provide social studies and management courses which are of broader interest.

....

Good Practice Example 12

The Chartered Institute of Housing issues the following guidelines on Equal Opportunities to everybody who is to be a tutor at one of its training events. These guidelines will also be of use to in–house trainers, and will be particularly helpful to people who do not usually work as tutors:

1. Please ensure that your language and material does not involve direct or indirect stereotyping of any groups. Racism, sexist, anti–disabled or otherwise discriminatory language or material should not be used.

2. Sentence construction should not be specific to one sex.

3. When using examples of case studies, please create positive images, e.g., women directors.

4. Avoid racist, sexist or sexually orientated jokes, even those considered mild or commonplace.

5. Please encourage participation by all delegates, particularly those who have difficulty expressing themselves and asking questions.

6. Please use the term 'black' when referring to ethnic groups unless individuals' preference for an alternative is made known. The term 'colour' causes offence and should not be used.

7. People with AIDS should be referred to as such and not as 'AIDS victims' or 'AIDS sufferers'.

8. We ask you to challenge any racist or sexist remarks made by delegates. You will need to use your judgement and respond appropriately in this situation.

9. You are asked to respect the confidentiality of any information given by course participants.

5.4.7 Management Development

Management development is a systematic approach to training and developing existing and potential managers in the organisation. The long term objective is to keep the organisation supplied with high calibre managers.

Increasingly the importance of this is being recognised in local authorities and housing associations. Any good training plan will have a section covering management development and Training Officers will wish to refer to the management competences drawn up by the Chartered Institute of Housing as part of the housing National and Scottish Vocational Qualifications scheme (see Appendices 2 and 4).

5.5 Apocryphal Housing Association's in–house training policy

Apocryphal Housing Association decided at an early stage of developing its training policy that it would train in–house whenever possible. Its training policy states:

AHA will conduct as much of its training programme in–house as is possible in order to encourage staff to share their experience and knowledge with colleagues and to ensure that the training budget is used to best effect. To achieve this, the Research And Development Manager will:

- organise regular training sessions for all line managers on training methods, presentation skills, equal opportunities and any other topics which will help them with their training function

- provide training and support to any staff member who is required to act as a trainer on a regular or occasional basis

- research and disseminate information within AHA on in–house training ideas and best practice from elsewhere

- set up a library of training materials, including videos, books, and training packages, for which a budget will be allocated. These materials will be loaned to staff as required

- develop an induction package to be used by new staff under the direction of the line managers

- book people on external training events only when the responsible manager confirms that training of an equal value cannot be provided in–house

- carefully monitor and evaluate all in–house training activities, reporting annually to Committee on ways to improve effectiveness.

This policy will be reviewed annually.

Chapter 6
Monitoring and evaluating training

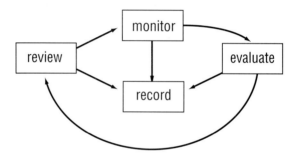

6.1   Introduction

Good training management, in common with other aspects of housing management, requires systematic monitoring and evaluation in order to check that agreed objectives are being achieved and that resources are not being wasted or misdirected.

Monitoring means keeping a record of the training conducted, the people and costs involved and the outcomes, with reference to the current training plan and training policy. It also requires a mechanism for ensuring that the results of the monitoring process are reviewed and fed back into the planning cycle so that lessons are learned and adjustments made. Evaluation is the assessment of the total costs and total benefits of each piece of training. The outcomes of the evaluation process are fed back into the monitoring system.

These aspects of training management are vital. It is important that the systems devised should not be so complicated and time consuming that they are disproportionate in effort or cost to the training itself and therefore likely to be skimped. The aim should be to keep everything as simple as possible whilst achieving the desired results. This chapter sets out the main parameters for a monitoring system and then describes some straightforward evaluation techniques which can be used by a non–specialist.

6.2   What to monitor

Items to be monitored should be spelled out in the organisation's training policy. At a minimum, monitoring will usually include:

- the number and type of training events actually held during the year
- training expenditure against budget
- uptake of training. This category might be broken down into uptake by:
  - department or section
  - male/female
  - ethnic origin
  - grade of staff
- the number and type of training opportunities provided against those requested by individuals or sections
- results of evaluations
- success in meeting any specific training targets (e.g. all new employees to complete induction training within 3 months of joining).

6.3   How to monitor

Some of the information, particularly expenditure and evaluation results, will be collected routinely as part of the whole training management cycle and monitoring will simply be a matter of collating and interpreting the data. Other topics will need to have appropriate mechanisms set up for recording the information required.

There is no reason why the Training Officer should do all the monitoring personally. For example, figures on the uptake of training are often best collected by section/department managers or by individual trainers and then passed on to the Training Officer for collation. The Training Officer will, however, have to ensure that all the monitors know what is required and should also set time–scales for the collection and return of information.

It is helpful to have standard forms for the monitoring process. This will ensure that information is collected systematically and recorded in the same way by different people. When designing the forms it is important to be disciplined about what information is needed and what it will be used for: it is very tempting to ask people to spend unnecessary time providing information which just might come in useful (but probably won't!).

6.4   Training records

The monitoring process will need to draw on records of all aspects of the organisation's training policy and practice. Equally, some of those records will be updated in the course of monitoring and review.

Training records should be:

- comprehensive

- systematic

- easy to read and use

- regularly updated

- regularly checked for accuracy by a third party or parties

- accessible to people who need to use them or have a right to see them

- stored securely when they contain confidential material about individuals

- cross–referenced to other relevant documents.

- labelled with the name of the organisation and given a title, document reference, date of issue and distribution list.

The training records will usually include:

- the organisation's training plan
- the organisation's training policies and objectives
- the training budget documentation
- copies of individual employee's training plans (if they are used)
- copies of any training needs assessments
- copies of standard monitoring forms
- evaluations with a record of any follow–up action taken
- useful information such as lists of trainers, training establishments and venues
- records of training reviews.

Training records should be subject to the same processes of document control as apply to other management records.

6.5 Why evaluate training?

It is important to check that the training budget is being used effectively because resources are always limited. In housing organisations there will be a direct relationship between the services which are provided to customers and the amount of money spent on staff training. As, in all probability, the training budget will be largely funded by rents, the organisation must be sure that ultimately there will be a clear cut benefit to the customer arising from the training.

The systematic evaluation of training also gives the message to employees that training is something which is taken seriously and valued by the organisation, not something to be regarded as a chore or an opportunity to go shopping!

Finally, proper evaluation of individual pieces of training will itself be a learning exercise. The organisation will know which trainers and training methods work well and which need some adjustment. The information gained can be fed back into the cycle of planning, implementation and evaluation.

> *"I remember one particular two–day course which was part of my training as a trainer. It was terrible! The trainer kept giving us lengthy tea and coffee breaks and then said we had worked so hard we could take a half day off – and our employers were paying for this! We were not asked to evaluate the training and so I wonder if that man is still being paid for teaching such bad practice."*

6.6   What are you evaluating?

Quite simply, you want to find out whether the time and effort put into each piece of training has been worthwhile. Specifically, you want to be sure that the individual training events meet their objectives and that the total training plan is meeting the needs of the organisation.

Since the organisation is no more and no less than the sum of the people within it, you must also evaluate the effect of training on them. All training is intended to bring about changes in knowledge, skills and attitudes in some combination. The evaluation process is in part an attempt to measure the changes in an individual's attitiudes, amount of knowledge, and/or level of skill as a result of training.

6.7   Evaluation measures

There are four, frequently used measures of the effectiveness of training; validation, cost, cost effectiveness and cost benefit. They each measure slightly different aspects and are best used in combination.

6.7.1 Validation

This requires a series of questions:

- what were the objectives of the training?
- did it meet those objectives?
- given the objectives of that particular piece of training, was it the right choice in terms of meeting the organisation's wider training objectives?

6.7.2 Cost

Real costs are greater than simply what has to be paid to the trainer. The calculations are relatively straightforward if the training was costed as part of the process of drawing up the training plan and the decisions about how to handle internal costs have already been made.

The remaining question is whether the training did actually cost the amount anticipated and if not, why not?

6.7.3 Cost effectiveness

This requires an assessment of value for money. Could you have achieved the same by spending less? For example, would it have been more cost effective to have run a day's course in–house rather than send six employees to a seminar in London?

6.7.4 Cost benefit

This is the most difficult measure because there will always be an element of subjectivity involved.

The Training Officer will need to make a judgement about whether the total benefit derived from the training justified the total costs involved. The 'total benefits' sum should take into account more than the achieving of immediate objectives. For example, did the trainee experience a boost in confidence as result of passing a course? Or, now that the assistant manager is familiar with the software used by the arrears section, will the money previously spent on consultants be saved in the future?

It will not always be possible to put a monetary value on benefits. Sometimes it is helpful to consider the costs of *not* training. As the old adage has it, if you think knowledge is expensive, try ignorance! In the examples above, the costs of not having an in–house software expert can be readily quantified by looking at the past costs of the alternative – buying in consultancy time. It is harder to put a value on boosting someone's confidence but it might help to think about the costs of replacing a member of staff who leaves because he feels unable to cope.

It is usually helpful for the Training Officer to discuss the total benefits with other people, particularly the trainees themselves and their managers. This can be done informally or in a structured way.

Evaluation framework

The Local Government Management Board proposes the following six stage framework for evaluating the effectiveness of management development. The framework is equally applicable to the evaluation of other forms of training and is particularly useful because of the way it links training evaluation with the work and development of the organisation.

1. Review organisational needs
How must the authority develop to meet the challenges it faces?

2. Identify management development needs and set objectives
What are the management development needs resulting from new organisational needs?

3. Plan and implement the management development approach
Did the approach fulfil stated aims and objectives for the individual and the organisation?

4. Change in the individual's behaviour and attitudes
Did learning take place and did behaviour on the job change?

---

5. Change in the organisation's performance
Have changes in individual behaviour contributed to organisational change?

6. Deliver services, meet objectives, respond to and anticipate change
What is the impact on the organisation's services and objectives? What is the impact on its capacity to respond to the environment and anticipate change?

Local Government Management Board (1993), *Valuing Management Development: Guidelines for Evaluating its Impact on Your Organisation.*

6.8   Evaluation methods

The evaluation process begins pre–training, can continue whilst the training is in process, and concludes at the end of training (although not necessarily immediately afterwards).

6.8.1 Pre–training evaluation

It might seem contradictory to say that the evaluation begins before the training, but it should do! Before the training starts:

- the Training Officer should ensure that the objectives are clearly defined and that they fit the organisation's training plan. It is then essential to decide the criteria for evaluation and the methods to be used. Everybody who will be involved in the evaluation (including the trainer) will have to be briefed on what is expected of them

- the trainee should have a meeting with the Training Officer or the line manager. At that meeting they should discuss the reason for the training, the objectives of the training and the expectations of the trainee, the standard expected of the trainee (and the standards may vary between individuals on the same training programme), the evaluation and the practical arrangements, including the budget.

"One man came into the room looking surly and when I asked everyone in turn how this training would help them in their work, he said he had no idea. Apparently he had been off sick and had come in that morning to find a note on his desk telling him to come to the training room at 10 o'clock. He had no idea why he was here, couldn't see how the topic related to his work and very much wanted to be somewhere (anywhere!) else. He was a real pain all day."

6.8.2 Evaluation during the training

There are two schools of thought about this. On the one hand it seems sensible, particularly on a long training programme, to make some evaluation of its effectiveness in teaching what it was intended to teach before the end, so that changes may be made if necessary. If you get to the end of an expensive piece of training and then discover that it did not meet its objectives it is too late to do anything about it!

On the other hand, some trainers believe that the only true test of the effectiveness of training is subsequent performance on the job, therefore assessing on–course performance is irrelevant and possibly misleading. They also argue that evaluation during the course of training, particularly if the trainer is required to comment on the trainee's performance, can prevent trust building up between trainer and trainee and this can itself interfere with the learning process.

For the Training Officer the best answer will usually be to discuss these issues with the trainer when the training is first being planned. In the case of on–the–job training, the trainee's manager will have an interest and will probably be able to suggest appropriate mechanisms.

Any evaluation during a piece of training should take account of the following:

- is the person responsible for the conduct of the training fully aware of the mid–training evaluation which is required?

- has the trainee been told what to expect?

- will the criteria chosen really test whether the training is meeting its objectives and making a real contribution to the development of the organisation?

- are the targets set for the trainee, in terms of knowledge gained, skills learned or attitudinal changes sought, achievable whilst providing sufficient challenge?

- making the necessary practical arrangement. For example, if the evaluation is to take the form of a written test of knowledge, who will mark the test and was there an initial test to act as a bench mark?

- doing the evaluation should be done at an appropriate stage of the training, perhaps at the end of a phase, rather than at an arbitrarily chosen time, say half way through

- it is better not to rely on a verbal report from either trainer or trainee, even if they have been given clear evaluation criteria, because their objectivity is likely to be influenced by whatever is going on in the training process at the time.

Good Practice Example 13

Kirklees Metropolitan Council uses a two–stage course evaluation form. The trainee completes the first part immediately after the course and hands it to the tutor. The second part is completed a few days after the course by the trainee and the trainee's supervisor.

Part A asks the trainee to assess the course's content, delivery and venue.

Part B asks about observed changes in the trainee, the team as a whole and the office environment. The final question asks about meeting further training needs and invites ideas for meeting them.

6.8.3 Post–training evaluation

The post–training phase of evaluation is the most important and it is never in the interests of the organisation to skip it, however pressing other tasks might be. There are a number of methods which can be used. The choice will depend on the nature of the training and, to an extent, the individuals concerned. In some cases a combination of techniques will be necessary.

It is at that this stage that the four measures of evaluation – validation, cost, cost benefit and cost effectiveness – need to be brought into use and the results analysed.

The four techniques which are described below are primarily concerned with validation in that they measure the success of the training in meeting its own internal objectives and in contributing to the organisation's wider objectives. They are all commonly used and each has its strengths and weaknesses.

(i)   Immediate evaluation by the trainee
There is increasing use of "smile sheets", assessment questionnaires which are completed by participants as soon as a training event is over. These have their uses as an immediate source of feedback and comments, and are particularly valuable on the training process, for example, the venue and administration, rather than on the outcome of the training. They should not be regarded as sufficient evaluation on their own because they also have a number of drawbacks:

•   they are very subjective. Usually participants are asked to judge the quality of the trainer and the training but without the criteria having been spelled out. It is therefore difficult to be sure exactly what the evaluations mean, and to know how to interpret contradictory judgements

•   they are usually completed too soon after the event for the full impact of the training to be felt where it matters – at work. It is quite possible for someone to thoroughly enjoy a seminar, rate the trainers and the whole experience very highly, but then return to their work routine without ever making use of the information they were supposed to have gained. In such a case the training is wasted despite its positive assessment

- the "critical incident phenomenon" will affect people's judgement. That is, undue weight will be given to the last thing which happened.

(ii)   Debriefing by the manager

Immediately after a piece of training has been completed manager and trainee should meet to discuss the training process and its outcomes for the trainee. This form of evaluation should be a routine part of the organisation's training management and will be a natural follow–up to the pre–course meeting between trainee and manager.

At the debriefing the trainee and manager will want to evaluate the training in terms of the extent to which the training achieved its objectives and what the trainee actually learnt. Did the trainee achieve the targets which were agreed at the outset? If not why not? Conversely, did her/his performance exceed expectations to the extent that he/she is now going to find their job insufficiently challenging? The manager and trainee will also have to agree on how the new knowledge, skills or attitude learned will be reinforced in the workplace and on how they will be evaluated.

The information collected will be passed to the Training Officer for collation with other evaluation material. There will also need to be some further action to update the trainee's training record and plan.

··

Good Practice Example 14

The Chartered Institute of Housing gives seminar delegates an appraisal form which they are encouraged to complete and hand in to the organisers at the end of the day.

Delegates are asked to rate each of the contributors on a 5 point scale ranging from Excellent to Poor. They are asked to answer the following:

- were there any topics which you feel should have been included which did not appear on the programme?

- were there any topics which you feel should have been omitted or reduced?

- is there anything we could have done to make the day better organised?

- did you find the venue satisfactory?

- did you find the catering satisfactory?

- what would you like to see the Institute do as a follow–up to this Seminar?

- Comments...

....

(iii)　Project work

This is a form of training evaluation by proxy. As the purpose of training is to increase competence at work, the effectiveness of a training programme can sometimes be evaluated by requiring the trainee to complete a project which is designed to test the extent to which they have acquired the knowledge or skills which the training was intended to teach. The advantages of this evaluation method are:

- it requires the active involvement of the trainee who has a chance to demonstrate new competencies

- the results are directly related to the trainee's work and are (should be!) of obvious benefit to the organisation.

The main disadvantage is that it does require a considerable commitment by the responsible manager who will have to think of an appropriate project (unless the trainer is able to do this), oversee the conduct of the project and then evaluate the results. Then there will probably need to be follow up action, perhaps in the form of further training for the employee. If the manager is not able or willing to carry all this through, the training cannot be properly evaluated and there is a danger that the trainee will feel that the whole exercise was a waste of time.

The completion of the project should show up strengths and deficiencies in the particular piece of training which is being evaluated. These will have to be recorded and the necessary action taken.

(iv)   Action Plans

This method of evaluation works on similar principles as evaluation by project and shares that method's strengths and weaknesses. Again the idea is to evaluate the success of the training in terms of its effect on the trainee's performance at work.

In the pre–training briefing, the application of the training to the job is discussed and the trainee reminded to keep possible applications in mind during the training. After the training the trainee draws up a personal action plan which applies what was learned in the training by setting specific goals to be achieved at work. The action plan is then discussed by the trainee and manager at the post–training briefing and time–scales are set. Together the manager and trainee monitor progress towards achieving the goals, recording any difficulties which suggest that the training did not achieve its objectives or which show a need for further training.

(v)   Surveys

Under certain circumstances, surveys conducted a little after training has finished are useful evaluation tools. Good Practice Example 15 shows how York City Council made use of surveys, plus other techniques, in the evaluation of its Training Hour, a long term training scheme.

··

Good Practice Example 15

An Evaluation of York City Council Housing Services' Training Hour.

The York Housing Services Training Hour was set up, initially on a trial basis, to meet the following objectives:

- to address stated training needs of staff including new members of staff
- to enhance staff morale
- to mix staff from different sections and so 'break down barriers'
- to ensure staff are more aware of corporate objectives and department plans and policies.

At the end of the trial period the Director was able to put a paper to Committee which evaluated the success of the Training Hour in terms of each objective. The evaluation methods used included surveys of customers, managers and staff.

An indication of the thoroughness of their approach is the fact that the telephonists monitored the number of telephone calls received whilst the department was closed for the Hour, so that the impact on services to the customers could be evaluated.

The report to Committee said of the third objective:

> *"it is important that staff from different work groups understand what each is doing in order to ensure that they appreciate each other's part in providing housing services to customers... In a survey conducted in October, 63% of staff state that Training Hour sessions have helped in this respect. An analysis of attendance at Training Hour sessions demonstrates that staff from different work groups have mixed, which has had a positive benefit on breaking down barriers between sections and encouraged staff to understand the work of their colleagues. For example, Estate Managers have attended sessions on allocations policy and Maintenance staff have attended Housing Needs sessions."*

Attendance at the Training Hour was monitored on a weekly basis so that the Department knew how many staff had attended and how many training hours in total had been provided.

The surveys also gave a number of ideas for improving the Training Hour. These were put to Committee with recommendations for action. The Training Hour is now an established part of training provision in York's Housing Department and is gradually being introduced in other parts of the Council.

6.9   Evaluation – Pulling it all together

The Training Officer will usually be responsible for pulling together all the elements of evaluation and making effective use of the information gained. As a starting point there should be material from whatever validation techniques have been used and information on the actual costs of the training compared with the anticipated costs.

The Training Officer can consider the cost benefit and cost effectiveness of the training. At this stage it will be useful to consult all the "stakeholders", that is, all the people who have an interest in the training and its outcome. These might include :

- the trainer (if there was one)
- the trainee
- the trainee's manager or supervisor
- possibly a senior manager
- possibly a Committee Member with particular responsibility for training.

Just who the stakeholders are will vary from organisation to organisation and from one piece of training to another.

There are no hard and fast rules for the conduct of this final evaluation. In some cases it will be done by telephone or in a number of informal meetings, in others a formal meeting will be specially convened. Sometimes the people concerned will be asked to complete and return evaluation forms. The method used will reflect the nature and size of the organisation and the scale of the training under evaluation. It would not be cost effective for the evaluation to cost more than the training itself!

The most important stage of evaluation is putting the information gained and the decisions made to good use. If this is not done, much of the effort already put in will be wasted. The Training Officer will need to have a system for feeding the outcome into the organisation's training plan to inform the next round of decisions about objectives and training methods (see 6.10). There may also be adjustments to be made to the training budget to take account of an overspend or underspend and that and any other follow–up action should be done and noted. It will also be necessary to update the training records. Only when all this is done is the evaluation at an end.

6.10   Using the Results of monitoring and evaluation

The monitoring and evaluation of training is not an end in itself and all the effort put into it will be wasted if the findings are not used to review of the operational success of the training policies and training plan.

The organisation will almost certainly find it useful to have a summary of the monitoring information in the form of an annual report. The report should be written before the preparation of the following year's training plan so that the conclusions can be fed into the planning process. Some possible heading are:

- statement of current training policies with any particular objectives or targets

- summary of the year's training plan

- budget statement (actual expenditure against planned)

- summary of monitoring results (including evaluations)

- commentary on the extent to which policies were implemented and targets met

- lessons learned from successes and failures

- recommendations for the next planning cycle.

6.11   Apocryphal Housing Association's Training Needs Form

Apocryphal Housing Association's new Director has introduced a system of annual training needs reviews for every member of staff. In order for the information to be useful it was decided that it was important that it should be collected and presented in the same format by everybody. Therefore the Research Manager put time into devising a standard form.

The line managers are responsible for conducting these reviews within a given time span, completing the forms and then sending them to the Research Manager for action.

A typical Training Needs form, once completed, looks like this:

Apocryphal Housing Association
Annual Review of Staff Training Needs

Name and post of responsible Line Manager:
Mary McCarthy, Tenant Services Manager

Name and post of Staff Member:
Ian Brown, Area Housing Manager, West Area

Length of time in post: **Date of review:**
One month   12 January 1993

1. Training which would help you to be more effective in your current job:
A course on staff appraisal
Training in tenant participation – legislation, AHA's policies, techniques

2. Training which would help prepare you for promotion:
Introduction to business planning
General management training

3. General professional development:
Training on the effects of CCT on housing management
Homelessness legislation

4. Personal development training:
Stress control and time management.

5. Comments:
Ian and I agree that training in staff appraisal is a matter of urgency for him because of his new responsibilities in this post.
He has had no direct experience of working with tenants' groups and therefore also needs training in tenant participation in order to take this forward in West Area.

6. Signatures:
Manager: M.McCarthy   **Staff member:** Ian Brown

The Research Manager collects and collates these forms, updating the training records which are kept for each staff member. She is then responsible for deciding how best to meet the needs identified in the context of the training policy and budget and in the light of current operational priorities. The results of this assessment are then built into the draft training plan, and the Research Manager tells the line managers what training will be provided in response to the needs identified.

In AHA it is the Research Manager who is responsible for ensuring that all monitoring, evaluation and record keeping is carried out correctly.

Kirklees Metropolitan Council
Course evaluation form

Instructions
Please complete part a of this form immediately after the course and hand it to the tutor.

Part b should be completed a few days after the course in conjunction with your supervisor and returned to the tutor.

Part A   Course Details and Content

1   Course details

Course title/subject: _____

Tutor/s: _____

Venue: _____

Dates: _____

2   Participants details

Name: _____

Job title: _____

Place of work: _____

3. Course assessment

Please tick the column on the right which most nearly expresses your view on each question

		Yes	Mostly	Partly	No
A	Were the aim/objectives of the course explained to you? Were these met? Aim: Aim: Aim: Aim:				
B	Was the course relevant to your work?				
C	Did you find the material or content? Interesting Relevant Useful				
D	Was the course pitched at the appropriate level for you?				
E	Was the pace acceptable?				
F	Was the length of the course correct?				
G	Was the standard of presentation satisfactory?				
H	Was there a good mix of training methods?				
I	Was the amount of information sufficient?				
J	Was the quality of the information sufficient?				
K	Was the training venue satisfactory?				
L	Additional information				

Please use this part to amplify or clarify any of the answers given above and suggestions for improving the course.

Part B To be completed after the course in conjunction with supervisor

1   Comments
Please give your comments following the opportunity to reflect. What changes
if any have you observed: in yourself; in the team as a whole; in the office
environment? Do you feel the course was time well spent? Why?

---

2   Comments of supervisor
I have discussed both the course and the above observations with my staff
member, and make the following comments:

**3   What further training needs have you identified in this area? What ideas
do you have for meeting these?

Name _____

Position _____

Chapter 7
Summary

7.1   Preparing to manage training

Perhaps the single most important activity to be undertaken by any organisation is training the people who work within it. Good training will increase the effectiveness of individuals and teams, thus making the whole organisation more effective. The more changeable the environment in which the organisation operates, the more important it is to give people the knowledge, skills and attitudes they need in order to respond positively to change. Training is the key to successful adaptation and adaption is the key to organisational success!

In training as in other aspects of good management, thorough preparation and planning is necessary to avoid wasting time, money and effort. Even before a training plan is devised, any organisation needs to prepare by putting in place:

- a training policy which defines the organisation's intentions with regard to training

- a middle to senior manager whose job description includes specific responsibility for training management and who has had appropriate training

- a training budget.

7.2   Identifying training needs

Change, whether internal or external, creates a need for training. The person responsible for training (called the Training Officer throughout this handbook) must identify the organisation's needs and the needs of individual employees before drawing up a training plan designed to move the organisation forward. The training policy is useful during this process as it provides a framework and sets priorities.

The identification of need is best treated as a continuous process to be done on a systematic basis, not as a once and for all exercise. This encourages people to view training as an ongoing response to changing individual and organisational circumstances, not as a one–off activity.

7.3   Analysing needs and devising training plans

The organisation's training plan will reflect the organisation's current strategic priorities, such as preparation for CCT, as well as long term policies, such as the provision of induction training to all new staff and Committee members. Ideally, individuals will also have their own training plans, covering training for current and future job needs plus personal development. All plans should be costed and should incorporate a range of training methods.

The training plan is best issued as a consultation document initially, to help develop a sense of ownership at all levels of the organisation. The aim is to ensure that staff will be willing participants in the drive to move the organisation forward.

7.4   Learning and teaching in–house

Although external training events have an important place in training programmes, for many topics the provision of training in–house is more efficient than sending people away on courses. There is a variety of training techniques which can be used in–house, enabling training to be tailored to specific needs and circumstances. An understanding of the factors which help people to learn is helpful to everyone involved in training activities.

7.5   Monitoring and evaluating training

All training needs to be monitored and evaluated to ensure that it is effective. That is, the organisation must be certain that it is deriving maximum value from its training programme and that time, money and effort is not being wasted on activities or methods which are not as efficient as they might be. The fundamental questions which monitoring and evaluation should answer are:

- how have attitudes, knowledge and skills in the work place changed as a result of training?

- have our organisational objectives been met?

- how much has that change cost?

- could it have been done more effectively?

The process of monitoring and evaluation is itself a learning exercise and maximum benefit will be derived when the answers to these questions are used to inform the next round of planning for training.

Monitoring and evaluation will require record keeping. Training documents should follow the same principles as other management records; they should be kept to the necessary minimum, be written in simple language, be identifiable and regularly updated.

7.6   And finally...

To the non–specialist it may at first seem that training is a particularly complex activity with a language all its own! This handbook is intended to demystify some of the aspects of training management with which a training officer in a housing department or association should be familiar. There are many other sources of advice and assistance available and the Appendices provide factual information and useful contacts. Above all, it is helpful to remember that the good management practices which are applied to other aspects of the housing organisation's work apply equally to training management. Stick to the cycle of planning, delivery, evaluation and review and everything else should fall into place!

Appendix 1
The housing organisations which contributed to this handbook

The following housing associations and local authorities gave their time and energy to the development of the Good Practice Examples. We are very grateful for their contribution to this handbook. Although their structures for the delivery of training services differ, the positive commitment to training and development is common to all.

Bradford and Northern Housing Association
The Association which manages more than 8000 homes has its Headquarters in Shipley, West Yorkshire. The training service is delivered by a Training Section based in the Headquarters building. A team of six headed by the Training and Personnel Manager are responsible for the recruitment and training of 600 staff.

Delyn District Council
Delyn District Council, in the county of Clwyd, North Wales, has 4,400 units of housing. Delyn has a Training Officer within Personnel Services who is responsible for training the 100 housing staff as well as the other staff within the Council. A feature of the recent training work has been the completion of a training audit throughout the Housing Department.

Key Housing Association
Key Housing Association was set up in 1977 to provide accommodation in the community for people with learning difficulties and is now, with more than 600 units, the largest single provider of this kind of accommodation in Scotland. Key has projects scattered throughout Scotland, providing a mix of residential care, supported tenancies and flats and houses let unsupported to nominees from District Councils. There are some 300 project staff, spread from the far north of Scotland to Dumfries and Galloway, and they are supported by the office staff who are based in Glasgow. The responsibilities of the three full time members of the Staff Development Section include the planning and delivery of training.

Kirklees Metropolitan Borough Council
Kirklees is the second largest metropolitan council in England. The Council owns over 32,000 homes. The Training and Development unit works within Personal Services to provide training support to the Housing Service, Social Services and the other departments in the Resources section. Ten Training Officers and four support staff service the training requirements of the 500 staff in the Housing Department, as well as the staff in the other sections.

London Borough of Newham
The London Borough of Newham owns 27,000 homes, nearly one third of all the homes in the Borough. The Housing Department prides itself on its high performance and on having the one of the lowest rent levels in London. Housing management is decentralised and there is a central Housing Training Unit with a staff of four.

(Copies of Newham's CCT training strategy are available from the Principal Training Officer for a small fee to cover costs.)

Notting Hill Housing Group
Notting Hill Housing Group provides 10,000 homes of mixed tenure type in the London area. To meet the varying training needs of the Group's 400 staff, NHHG has a Training Section with four staff members. Their responsibilities include both planning for training and implementation of training programmes. Their task is complex because both Group training and training specifically geared to the needs of the Group's constituent parts are required.

Sedgefield District Council
Sedgefield District Council has a housing stock of 12,000 properties. The Training Section in the Chief Executive's Office plans and delivers training services to nearly 200 housing staff. In close co–operation with senior housing managers at Sedgefield, the Training Section has recently concluded a highly successful programme whereby specialist housing officers were trained to become generic local estate officers.

Stirling District Council
Stirling District Council has some 10,500 homes. There is one training officer, based in Central Support Services, who is responsible for training throughout the Council. Recent training intiatives have included a programme linking equal opportunities with customer care, using trainers from local voluntary organisations. Stirling is also using

cascade training on a programme for supervisors and potential supervisors.

York City Council
York manages about 10,000 homes. Training services for the 170 housing staff are planned and organised by the Customer Services Manager in the Housing Department. The Tenancies and Benefits Manager also handle some training responsibilities. York is noted for its innovative training programmes for its housing staff.

Individual contributions from these housing organisations have been invaluable. We particularly want to thank:

Chris Collins, Dawn Corbett, Kate Houchin, Loraine Kennedy, Carol King, Nigel Lower, Donald MacKinnon, Kathy Methven, Roy Wallington, Ian Wright.

Appendix 2
List of contacts for training advice and information

The Chartered Institute of Housing

For information on training events, services and publications contact the training sections:

The Chartered Institute of Housing
Octavia House
Westwood Way
Coventry CV4 8JP
Tel: 0203 695010

Chartered Institute of Housing in Scotland
6 Palmerston Place
Edinburgh
EH12 5AA
Tel: 031–225–4544

Chartered Institute of Housing in Wales
4th Floor
Dominion House North
Dominion Arcade
Queen Street
Cardiff
Tel: 0222–397402

The National Federation of Housing Associations

For information on their training programmes, services and publications contact:

National Federation of Housing Associations
175 Gray's Inn Road
London
WC1X 8UP
Tel: 071–278–6571

HERA Careers Service

Services on offer include:

- range of publications on housing training, education and careers
- information on housing training and education, including databases of training resources, a directory of housing trainers and a video library
- individual counselling in job seeking techniques and career planning
- partnership with Habitat Formation, a French housing training organisation.

Kate Hargreaves
HERA Careers Service
1st Floor, 2 Valentine Place
London SE1 8QH
Tel: 071–928–6147

The Industrial Society

Runs a variety of training events, provides consultancy and also produces publications. "Briefing Plus" is a monthly publication which focuses on management and training matters.

The Institute of Training and Development

Provides information, advice and an extensive library to members.

Institute of Training and Development
Marlow House
Institute Road
Marlow
Tel: 0628 890123

The Local Government Management Board

Can supply a range of publications related to training, with an emphasis on management. Periodicals include "Towards a Quality Workforce" and "what's on Tramis", both of which contain news and information about training developments and initiatives and an NVQ Housing Sector Newsletter.

Management Education and Training

For information about Crediting Competence, a work–related assessment of managers, contact:

The Local Government Management Board
Arndale House
Arndale Centre
Luton
Bedfordshire LU1 2TS
Tel: 0582 451166.

The Board has entered into a 'multi–site Crediting Competence Agreement' with the Management Charter Initiative for the whole of local government to offer a range of services both centrally from the Board and from Regional Offices/Employers' Organisations. For information about the Management Charter Initiative contact:

The National Forum for Management Education and Development
MCI
Russell Square House
10–12 Russell Square
London WC1B 5BZ
Tel: 071 872 9000.

Appendix 3
Routes into housing qualifications

This appendix provides details of the various housing qualifications available both from professional bodies and those provided by educational establishments.

The Professional Diploma (PD) is the most common form of vocational training undertaken by housing staff, administered by the Chartered Institute of Housing. Membership of the Chartered Institute most commonly requires that housing staff undertake a period of study at a college or institute of further education and complete a practical Test of Professional Practice (TPP). There are also accelerated routes for a small number of senior staff that do not require such study, but these are not commonplace.

There are two distinct study routes to qualifying for the Chartered Institute's professional qualification, as follows:

For non–graduates, there is a progression through the BTEC National Certificate in Housing Studies, spread over two years on a day release basis and aimed primarily at younger staff with some qualifications but limited work experience. A total of 37 colleges in England offer this course, as well as 3 colleges in Wales and 7 in Scotland.

For staff who have completed this course, or for others aged 18 and over who have some housing experience, the next stage is the BTEC Higher National Certificate in Housing Studies. This is also a two year day release course, during which staff must also complete the TPP stage 1, which is a practical test of students' ability to apply their housing knowledge to their work and involves, among other requirements, the completion of a logbook detailing their work experience and various case studies and reports. A total of 17 colleges in England offer this course, as well as 2 colleges in Wales and 3 in Scotland.

The final stage of the route to the PD for non–graduates is the Professional Diploma in Housing, which requires a further two years of study on a day release basis and the completion of the TPP stage 2.

For a non–graduate coming in at the BTEC National Certificate stage, a minimum of six years part–time study are therefore required before being eligible for the PD.

For graduates coming into housing, the routes to the PD involve first the Graduate Foundation Course in Housing, carried out on a day release basis over one year and requiring the successful completion of the TPP stage 1. A total of 8 colleges of further education offer this course in England, as well as one in Northern Ireland.

Students who successfully complete this course are at the same stage as those completing the BTEC HNC course as above and are eligible to study for the Professional Diploma in Housing. Graduates taking this route would therefore require a total of three years of part–time study before being eligible for the Professional Diploma.

There is an alternative route for graduates to the PD, namely by completion of a recognised post–graduate diploma in housing, which carry full exemption from the PD written examinations, although students must still complete the Test of Professional Practice. For full–time post–graduate students, the course takes two years, the second of which is spent on placement with a housing organisation, with occasional block teaching at their educational establishment as well. For part–time post–graduate students, the course lasts for three years on a day release or block release basis.

There is also a four year full–time course, including placements, for undergraduates on a number of housing courses which also carry exemption from the written PD examinations.

For further details of the PD, consult the Chartered Institute of Housing

The full time Post Graduate Diploma in Housing is funded by the Department of the Environment through Section 16 funding and is offered by 7 universities and polytechnics in England, 1 in Wales and 2 in Scotland. Five of these institutions in England also offer the part–time post graduate diploma, with a further 3 offering only the part time course. The undergraduate course in housing is offered by 5 institutions in England, 1 in Northern Ireland and 1 in Scotland (jointly run by two institutions).

The content of the courses provided, from the BTEC National Certificate to the Post Graduate Diploma in Housing, vary according to the ability of the students, but they share in common a range of core skills and subjects directly related to housing.

The Professional Diploma now offered by the CIH has been recently revised and restructured, in part in response to criticism from housing professionals that the old PD was inflexible and in many aspects irrelevant. The new PD has been designed so that any changes in course content can be made more readily in response to changing housing practice and policy. More significantly, the PD now also requires students to complete the two stage Test of Professional Practice, which ensure they have a thorough grounding in day to day housing work in a number of disciplines and is considered by housing professionals to provide a more realistic and challenging qualification.

Academic courses in housing are offered by a total of 12 universitiesj. The overwhelming majority of these courses are recognised by the CIH as carrying exemption in some degree from the written examinations for the PD, and some also carry exemption from the professional examinations of other housing related professional bodies such as the Royal Institute of Chartered Surveyors, the Royal Institute of British Architects and the Institute of Environmental Health Officers.

The courses have developed over the last few years in response to demands from both employers and prospective students, to provide staff with developed skills in housing as well as a committed and flexible approach to the field. The post graduate diploma courses, for example, aim to encourage amongst students a critical analysis of housing policies and related issues and the ability to examine social and economic aspects of housing from different perspectives. A typical course would include practical skills in social policy, housing law, building studies, housing finance, management studies and housing policy and administration.

The basic content and style of the courses, while addressing the core policy and management issues of relevance to housing staff, display variety in respect of their approach and style, reflecting close links established by the institutions with local employers and with the local and regional housing priorities and context.

Those courses that carry exemptions from the PD are all validated by the CIH on a regular basis, and once every five years at a minimum. This is a rigorous validation process which is undertaken by housing professionals active in the field, as well as representative bodies and external examiners. The purpose of the validation is to ensure that the requirements of the PD are met in full and that the courses retain a high standard and are relevant to current housing policy and practice.

Appendix 4
References and further reading

Applegarth, Michael (1992)
How to Take a Training Audit, Kogan Page, London.

Armstrong, M. (1988)
A Handbook of Personnel Management Practice, Kogan Page, London.
(Chapter 29, Training).

Department of the Environment (1994)
Education and Training for Housing Management, HMSO, London.
ISBN 0 11 752899 4

Lawson, Ian (1989, 3rd Edition)
Appraisal and Appraisal Interviewing, The Industrial Society, London.
ISBN 0 85290 412 6

The Local Government Management Board (1991)
Achieving Success: A Corporate Training Strategy, Luton.
ISBN 0 7488 9830 1.

The Local Government Management Board (1991)
On the Job Training: Guidelines for Managers, Luton.
ISBN 0 7488 9846 8

The Local Government Management Board (1993)
Managing Tomorrow, Panel of Inquiry Report, Luton.

The Local Government Management Board (1993)
Valuing Management Development: Guidelines for Evaluating Its Impact on Your Organisation, Luton.
ISBN 0 7488 9636 8

Local Government Training Board (1990)
Making Housing Work: with good training, Luton.
ISBN 0 7488 00026.

Local Government Training Board (1990)
Developing Managers in Housing Organisations, Luton.
ISBN 0 7488 0071 9

Newby, A. (1992)
Training Evaluation Handbook, Gower, London.

Robinson, Kenneth R.(1985, 2nd Edition)
A Handbook of Training Management, Kogan Page, London.
ISBN 1 85091 061 8.

Scott, Suzie (1993)
Educating for Training and Change, Institute of Housing in Scotland.